Mr. and Mrs. Personality

Understanding Your Own Personality to Create Better Relationships

By: Alvin Harper

9781680322477

PUBLISHERS NOTES

Disclaimer – Speedy Publishing LLC

This publication is intended to provide helpful and informative material. It is not intended to diagnose, treat, cure, or prevent any health problem or condition, nor is intended to replace the advice of a physician. No action should be taken solely on the contents of this book. Always consult your physician or qualified health-care professional on any matters regarding your health and before adopting any suggestions in this book or drawing inferences from it.

The author and publisher specifically disclaim all responsibility for any liability, loss or risk, personal or otherwise, which is incurred as a consequence, directly or indirectly, from the use or application of any contents of this book.

Any and all product names referenced within this book are the trademarks of their respective owners. None of these owners have sponsored, authorized, endorsed, or approved this book.

Always read all information provided by the manufacturers' product labels before using their products. The author and publisher are not responsible for claims made by manufacturers.

This book was originally printed before 2014. This is an adapted reprint by Speedy Publishing LLC with newly updated content designed to help readers with much more accurate and timely information and data.

Speedy Publishing LLC

40 E Main Street, Newark, Delaware, 19711

Contact Us: 1-888-248-4521

Website: http://www.speedypublishing.co

REPRINTED Paperback Edition: ISBN: 9781680322477

Manufactured in the United States of America

DEDICATION

I dedicate this book to my family. My family is simply the source of my strength and my inspiration.

TABLE OF CONTENTS

Chapter 1- Find Your Own Identity, Find Your Own Personality

There are many people that have issues in their life. They may have to find a way to take on the good and the bad things that can come up in the everyday life that they lead. Sometimes the hard times are very depressing and can cause us to lose sight of what we have to do in life. There are many people that have to turn to therapy for help in these situations. This is nothing to be ashamed about or to be upset over. If therapy is something that can help you live a better life and grow as a person, you should do it.

Getting out of the rut that a person is in is very important for personal growth. You can guarantee that you will never move past the hard times if you do not find out what is causing the grief and hardship in your life. If you do take the time to go through therapy and get help for your problems, you will be able to move past all of it and get on to better and bigger things.

If you are not sure what therapy can do for you, you may want to speak to someone that has already been through it. You might want to ask others how this form of treatment has helped them become better people and able to have personal growth in their lifetime. This is something that can really help you achieve your goal of getting to where you want and need to be in life. You have to make the right choices so that you are able to have the life that you were meant to have.

Therapy can help you work through your issues and get you to where you have to be so that you can find happiness. You will see that there are many forms of therapy and you must make sure that you have the right method for the situation that you are in. When you are able to understand where your problems are coming from, you will be able to move on and get on to growing as a person like you need to be. You will be able to experience new and more exciting things. You will also be able to express yourself better and this will help you find more friends and have all that you need in your life.

Getting to where you want and need to be in life is something that may take some time. You have to be patient and also be willing to explore why and what are the main reasons behind your problems. If you are willing to take time to learn more about who you are and what you need in life, then you are willing to give yourself the chance to grow as a person and to become the adult that you want to be. Therapy is something that is going to be making you see what you need to in order to be happy and satisfied in your personal growth and your everyday environment.

When you are just not sure about things in your life, you may want to have some form of therapy to get the answers that you are looking for. Therapy is something that you can do in private and no one needs to know about it. This is something that you can do for a short time of long term depending on the problems and the issues that you are having at the time. You will want to use therapy as a way to find out more about yourself and how you want to live your life in the future.

How to use technology to increase personal growth and fulfillment

There are so many amazing things that you can do today because of technology. You can do just about anything that you have ever dreamed about and more. There are things that are being invented everyday that are made to help us throughout our daily lives. There are also things to help us become better people too. We can actually lean from the technology that is being brought to us all the time. We can grow as a person and learn from what these things bring to us.

Technology is a great thing. There are many great ideas that are brought to us to make our live better and more exciting. We can learn from all the things that we have through technology. These things are used to make life interesting too. We can see a whole new world through what technology brings to so and us much more. Giving our self-personal growth is going to be one of the best things that we can do for our own good interest. We have to be willing to grow and move on to better and bigger things. There is no room for us to be stuck in the past and not willing to experience new and more adventurous things.

We all have to move on to other things at some point in our life. We have to be willing to make our goals come true. When we are able to bring technology to our life, we are going to widen our view to what we can do in life and what our possibilities are. Getting where we want to and need to be in life is something that is so exciting and with the right tools we can get there with no problem.

Computers and the Internet are just a few of the forms of technology that is making it easy for us to move on to more exciting and new things each day. We are able to use these things to get to just about anywhere in the world and find out almost anything that we want to know. This is so important when it comes to what we want to have in life. This is very important for us to so that we are able to grow into the people that we want to be. Personal growth is a great form of self-improvement as well.

There are also a lot of new and great tools that are helping us find out about where we want to go and what we want to do in life. We are able to move on to the things that are important to us and that we want to know more about because of what technology has brought us. We are able to use the resources that we have in front of us so that we can do more things that make us happy. This is a great method of personal growth and experience as well. You cannot ask for more when it comes to getting where you want to be in life and what you think that you deserve as well.

You should not be afraid of what technology has to offer for you. You should embrace it and go with the flow. You are adding more excitement and more knowledge to your life as well. You will love the fact that you are able to improve your skills and your goals with the help that technology brings to your life. This is an amazing thing that can make anything possible for you.

Chapter 2- Personality Needs to be Nurtured

Today is a very busy world. There are more and more people stepping out and getting career of their own and doing what they want to in life. They are going to college and getting degrees, earning lots of money and they may or may not have families at home waiting one it. However, there are also a lot of stays at home moms that are making all of their dreams and goals come true as well. They are living the dream that they have had for a long time and feeling great about it.

Many people believe that if you are a stay at home mom, this must mean that you are lazy or stupid. However this is not the case at all. This is a silly misunderstanding and one that should be corrected very quickly. Being at home and raising a family is a very hard job. It is just as hard as any career that some other women may have. At times, being a stay at home mom can even be a little bit harder because of all the things that you they must do.

Mr. and Mrs. Personality

There are many women that want to stay home and take care of their children. They may want to make sure that they are taking care of their children and helping them grow as people. They want to make sure they are growing the way that they should and doing what is important for them at the same time. This is a goal that a woman should be proud of and take to heart. Staying at home and raising a family is a lifelong dream that can mean amazing and wonderful things. It can mean that a woman can do what she has always dreamed of doing and still be completely satisfied and happy too.

Being happy with your life is something that you should be proud of. You want to have personal growth that you can feel great about and know that you have achieved on your own. There is nothing wrong with wanting to be a stay at home mom and raise your children with the morals and the goals that you want them to have. You will find that this is a very rewarding job that can offer you a lifetime of great feelings and personal strength as well. You will appreciate the fact that you are an important role model in the children's life and you are giving them the balance and stability that they need to feel good.

There are many people that do not understand what being a stay at home mom means. They are not sure what the purpose of staying at home all day long really is. However, making sure that our children and family is well organized and well taken care of is something that any woman should feel good about. They should be proud that they have taken the time for their family that is needed and doing what makes them happy as well.

Women need to do what is right for their family and for themselves as well. When raising a family, it is essential that women also realize that they have to do what is good for them too. They have to have time for themselves and do the things that they like as well. This is something that will allow them to have personal growth and also relax and feel good about who they are and what they are doing with their life. Many women know what they have to do and how to get to this point in their life too. When a woman knows that she is doing the best that she can for her and her family, she is going to feel great about all the choices that she has made and continue to do well in her life.

How to find personal growth, as you find new friends

When you are looking to meet new people and make more friends you are actually expanding your own personal growth. This is something that many people should do for themselves. This will give them added confidence and more structure in their life as well. It is something that a person can grow from and use as a learning experience.

The more friends that we have in life will mean that the more fun and excitement we have as well. Then it is better to have too many friends than not enough. If you are looking to have the feeling that you belong and that you are important, you will see that you can get this from your friends. When you are sure that you have the support that you need, you will have a better time in life.

Growing as a person is something that we learn to do every day. There are many people that want to meet new people so that they can feel good about themselves. They want to make sure that they have wide variety of people that they can depend on when they need them. This will make you feel good and give you the strength that you are looking for so that you can have a normal and happy life.

You can meet friends just about anywhere. If you work, you may have already made lasting friendships there. This is a great way for you to meet new people as they are employed and you will have friends that you will have for a lifetime. You will also find that the more activities that you are in means that you will meet more and more people. You will see that you can make a lot of great friendships when you belong to clubs or other social organizations. These are people that will help your personal growth.

Finding new friends does not mean that you have to give up the old ones. There is no reason why you cannot combine the old and the new friends together. In fact, this is a great way for you to have a good experience in your personal growth. You can have friends for different reasons and you will want to share as much time with them as you can. This will help you to keep your personal ties with the special bonding friends and you will also be able to keep in touch with your everyday social friendships as well.

Making friends is part of life. Sometimes you will make friends that you will not have for very long and other times; you will make friends that you have for a lifetime. No matter how long you keep them in your life, you are still giving yourself a great way of personal growth. This is something that you can do for yourself to make it easier to go through life and get the things that you want. Each friend can offer you something new and exciting to bring to your life.

You will defiantly experience some hard times when you have friends. You will go through good times and bad. However, the best thing that you can do is make sure that you have the ability to make sure that you are using each friendship as a personal growth experience so that you can grow as a person and have a better life ahead of you. Friends are a part of your growing experience and everyone will want to make a least one really good friend in their life. Having friends makes you stronger and happier and will give you the important things in life.

It is important to take time out of your busy life to make friends so that you can get the support and love that you need in your life. Friends will make you grow and give you the personal growth that you need to have a happy life.

How to find personal growth through education

Education is one of the most important things that you can have in life. This is something that you will want to think about so that you are able to achieve the goals in life that you want and need. You want to make sure that you have the education that will get you where you need to be in life. This will give you what you need for your own personal growth. You will feel better and be able to improve your skills for things that you want in life.

Education is a great tool. No matter what you want to be or do in life, you will want to have education. This is something that will make your life fuller and better so that you can be prepared for the road ahead of you. Having personal growth through education is a great way to give your self-pride and self worth so that you are able to do what you want to in life. There are many reasons why you should get a good education, however the best reason is for yourself.

If you are thinking about doing one certain job in your life you will want to make sure that you are getting the right education. You need to be aware of all the great things that you can accomplish through education. Doing what makes you happy in life is most important. However, you will need to make sure that you have the right education so you can do this. You may be required to go to school for a certain length of time to get the personal growth that you is looking for.

If you are not sure what you want to become in life, you may want to take some time to think about this. You will need to be sure that you have the ability to do what you need to so that you have all the knowledge that is needed to get to this point. You will have to put a lot of effort into this so that you are getting what you need to. When you are prepared and have all the tools that are needed, you will see that you can be a stronger and more efficient person. You can watch as your personal growth expands and you are a happier and well-balanced person.

Getting your education is easy. All you have to do is make sure that you are doing what you need to so that you are fully aware of your options. When you have the proper tools and the right guidance, you can make your dreams come true and have a better shot at keeping your personal growth where you want it to be.

The main thing in education is to make sure that you are keeping up with the things in life that you want. You need to go after your goals in life so that you are growing inside more and more every day. The more room that you have to grow means that you will have more abilities and you can do more things in your lifetime. This is an amazing way to be a better person and make things happen for you. You will be able to make your goals and dreams in life happen for you and the people around you.

You have to be willing to create a great environment for you so that you can advance and make your life what you want it to be. You should think about the things that you like to do and this will help you with your own personal growth and get you where you need to go. Education is something that you need to do for your own personal growth so that you are able to do what you want to in life. The more that you know means that you will have a better time at getting to where you want to be. Education is a great way to move on to bigger and better things in your life.

How to Find personal growth using goals

It is not always easy to achieve our goals. We may have to keep reminding ourselves to stay on track. If you have tried to set goals and find that they are hard to work at, you may want to change your perspective. You have to remember that goals are an important part of personal growth. We must make goals for ourselves so that we can improve our life and stay on the right path.

There are many things that can kick us off track for our personal growth and goals. We may find that influences in our life and other people can have us to the point where we think that our goals are not as important as we think they are. We have to keep in mind that we need to stay on the right track so that we can keep motivated and keep on going in the right direction. This is the best way to make sure that we are still thinking about where we want to be and what we want to have in life.

If you get off course, you have to find a way to put yourself back on the right road. This will give you the ability to get back to where you need to be. It is a good feeling when you have the goals set so that you are making something of your life. You need to set at least three primary goals in your lifetime. These are the goals that you want to have done before you die. They are important so that you are able to make dreams come true and get more in personal growth.

It is not impossible to make goals for yourself. You need to think about what is important in your life and what you believe is going to be beneficial to you and your life. This is going to be up to you to get your priorities set so that you can meet all of your dreams and goals. There are many pressures in life and these things can make it hard to keep your focus on what is truly important to you and your life. You need to maintain your goals and stay on track so you are not pushing your dreams to the back burner in life.

You can keep track of the things that you want to do in life on paper. This is going to be a good way to remember what you think is important. You can use this as a method of staying on track and keeping your focus in life. You should remember what is going to be important to you in the long run. Once you have these things set in place, you will be able to put your goals out in front of you and start working on them one at a time.

Make note of the more important goals in life and what you need to work on. When you are sure of the things that you need to put first in your life, you will then be able to move on to the secondary goals that you want to accomplish. You do not have to make these goals come true in any amount of time. You can work on them and have them done as time goes, but as long as you have a list that is allowing you to remember all the things that you want in life, you will be on the right road.

Putting high standards on your list is another good way to stay on track. You can make sure that you are thinking about what you want to do and all that is important to you. When you have your goals in place and you are headed in the right direction, you can make your dreams and goals are a part of your personal growth for a better and brighter future. It is also important to make sure that no one stands in your way for attempting to complete any goals that you have set for your life.

How to achieve personal growth lessening stress

Stress is a terrible problem with just about everyone. There is no one that I can think of that does not have to deal with stress in some way or another. Usually everyone has to figure out a way to get over stress. They have to find a way to have it in their life and still be able to get past it. This is something that we all have to learn to do so that we can live a happier and healthier life as well.

We do not have to allow stress to ruin our life. We can have a more simple life if we just learn to handle stress and keep it to a minimum when we can. This is something that we have to learn to do to keep our sanity and to allow others to keep their sanity as well. You have to know what is important in life and what to let go. You do not have to get all worked up over certain things because they are just not worth it. You are damaging your health and your well being when you are getting all worked up over the smallest little thing.

The way that you achieve personal growth in your life is by the way that you handle your life. You have to know when to do things in your life and when not to. If you are getting upset over things that others are doing, you have to know when to let it go. You should not allow these things to make your life miserable. You need to put what is important in your life and use this good method of treatment. You need to use your positive goals and put them into place so that you are able to move on with your life.

Stress is a very powerful thing. You have to be willing to move past it and get yourself on a different road. When you are able to make the most of your life and what you want to do, you should think about the importance of everything that you are doing in your life. You need to find ways to relax so that you can do more important things and be a much happier person as well. There is nothing wrong with having a little bit of stress, however if you think that it is consuming your life, you have to find a way to get a hold of your life.

Mr. and Mrs. Personality
Stress is something that can turn your world upside down if you allow it to. You do not want to let this get you down. Think of things that you can do either alone or with others to get to where you want to be. You do not have to worry about anything if you are prepared. Being prepared is one of the better ways that you can move onto the right direction so that you are not dealing with stress. When you have everything planned out and ready to go, you are going to be doing yourself a big favor and this will allow you to move on past the hard things and get motivated for the good.

It is all about how you take things and how you see your life. If you are serious about being a better persona and using your personal growth as a way to get where you want to be, you will try and eliminate as much stress as you can. This is going to be a good way for you to make things better and to be a more complete in the things that you do with your life. You want to grow as a person so that you are able to enjoy the things that life has for you.

CHAPTER 3- LOVE YOUR OWN PERSONALITY BEFORE LOVING SOMEONE ELSE'S

Confidence is not something that comes easy to most. It is an emotion that has to be learned. You need to know what you can do to increase your personal confidence and how it can affect the way that you act and feel towards certain things in life. You need to think about what you can do to make your life better and what you need to do to boost up your self-esteem at the same time.

You should not worry about what other people think about you all the time. However, this is hard. You may not always be able to do this. It is difficult to move past the bad things that people do and say about us and we may have to find a way to get the confidence that is lost back. You can make your self-esteem grow if you have the right tools to do it with. You might have to let go and move on past these harsh words but it is the one thing that will get you where you need to be.

Mr. and Mrs. Personality
You need to learn to stand tall and be proud of who you are. When you are willing to feel good about who you are and what you are doing you will see the way that your emotional well being changes. You will notice a difference in the way that you act and the way that you feel in certain situations. You do not have to allow others to bring you down anymore. There is a way to move past this and to get to where you want and need to be.

You have to be able to allow yourself to grow from the inside out. You need to cleanse your body of the bad thoughts and allow them to be replaced by good ones. You are the only one that can determine your future. You need to put your own well being and emotions first so that you can achieve your goal of being more confidants and more in control of the things that matter most to you.

If you are looking for ways to boost your self-confidence, you can start by the people that you are associating with. You need to put yourself in good company. When you around people that make you feel good and care about you, this is a great way to make your confidence level rise and to get you feeling good about whom you are and improve your personal growth as well. This is an amazing feeling that will make you happier and healthier as well.

Do something for yourself. You need to make sure that you are putting yourself first in life. You may simply need a new haircut, brighter lipstick or a new outfit to make you feel more confident in your life. This will give you the feeling that you are beautiful and that you deserve the very best. Others will see the way that you feel and they will give you respect that you want and need too.

You also need to make sure that you have the right career path that you want. If you are not happy with the career that you have, you might want to change it. You need to do something that you are good at and that makes you feel good as well. There is nothing better than having a job that is satisfying and makes your confidence level rise about what it once was. This is something that will give you the personal growth experience that you are looking for as well.

How to improve your personal growth and feel good about yourself

When it comes to your personal growth, you will find that your self esteem levels are connected. You have to have a good level of self-esteem for you to grow personally, but you sometimes also need to go through a lot to gain self esteem. There are so many things that you can do to make yourself feel good; however, you need to find positive ways to reinforce personal growth. You will need to some soul searching to find what it is that makes you happy. You will also need to set yourself some short and long term goals for you to grow and feel better about yourself.

When it comes to setting goals you need to really think about who you are, where you are going, and what you want to be. Once you have defined yourself you can begin to set goals. You should set little goals and have at least one a month so that you are continuously striving for something. The key to good goal setting is knowing that you can achieve them and having a game plan. If you set unrealistic goals for yourself, you will never grow or feel better about yourself.

You need to think about what you really want. Maybe you need materialistic objects to feel better about yourself; however, it could be simply things like moving on and standing independently when it comes to finances. When it comes to materialistic objects, you need to know that no amount of money in the world can make you have self esteem, but it is the achievement that you have to get that money. Like you can go for a promotion, knowing that you worked hard, even though there is the money increase, it's really about the promotion.

When it comes to your self esteem levels you will find that you will see yourself definitely when you start reaching your goals. However, even if you take a shot and you miss, you should never let your self esteem be affected. You grow from your mistakes and the next time you aim at a goal, you will know exactly what it takes to achieve it. You will be able to grow from the negativity by making it positive. Also, at one point, you are going to need to realize that this is who you are and that's okay. You need to be satisfied with who you are, but always reach for more so that you can grow. People grow from their own mistakes, as well as, other people's mistakes. You need to listen to those around you and take risks, but always be aware of how you feel about yourself.

The worst thing that you can do to feel better about yourself is to let things get to you. You need to stop hiding your feelings by overspending when you go shopping or by eating, or whatever you do to fix your emotions quickly. Nothing temporary can every make you feel truly better. It may hide your feelings for a little bit, but it cannot solve anything. You will need a support system. When you are feeling bad about yourself you need to go talk to someone who is going to be encouraging. Eventually you will be able to comfort yourself and that is what growth is truly about.

Always try to keep the positive things in your life and keep plenty of people who love and care about you around. They are your support system and sometimes everyone needs someone to lean on every now and then. With facing your issues and setting goals you can grow and learn. You will begin to feel better about yourself when you see how far you truly have come.

How to help others, while improving your personal fulfillment

Have you ever noticed that by doing a good deed that you feel personal fulfilled? That's why a lot of people will do some local charity or even give to goodwill. They feel personal fulfillment by helping someone who is less fornicate than themselves. Sometimes you will notice that it is hard to express your own feelings, but you can seek out someone and help them with a small problem, and then all of a sudden you find comfort. This is because you connected with someone and you felt less alone. If you are able to help someone, you will feel a lot better about yourself because of the happiness of another. Even the most selfish person can find personal fulfillment from helping others.

When it comes to helping out, you don't have to do much. All you have to do is come around give them some attention. If you notice someone who is lonely you could go and sit with them. If you work with someone who eats lunch all by themselves, if you go and sit down by them, they will begin to be more social after awhile and they will owe it all to you. A person's happiness comes from attention. There are too many people out in the world who feels like everyone has forgotten them or has ignored them. Even if you say hi to someone passing by, they will begin to feel better about themselves, like someone cares. If you can make someone feel better about themselves then you will feel better about themselves.

Then there are other ways to help a person. It not only takes your time and energy, but also materials and money. You can always go to a local soup kitchen and feed the homeless. You can go read a bedtime story to an orphan. You can also put yourself out by donating things that you have become accustom to. Things like clothes, food, money, can easily be given to some of your local charities. You are sacrificing things to help another and you can feel good about not being so selfish. You can actually grow by giving some of the things that you take for granted to the homeless or an orphanage. Then there are people who devote their entire lives to helping others.

There are people who take civil service jobs to help out others. You can become a firefighter, police officer, a social worker, or even an aid at the local shelter. You can take a lot of positions where you help someone. They say that if you are a social worker, if you ever touch one child, if you ever help just one child, you have succeed in life. Social jobs are not easy and can sometimes be very dangerous, but they are also the most fulfilling jobs that one can ever have. If you find ways to incorporate helping people into your career, you will become very content with your life and with yourself. That's why many people become doctors, lawyers, nurses, and so one because they are providing not just a service, but they have a job where they can help people. By helping people you become fulfilled.

If you are able to identify with someone, you will find that you can also feel fulfilled. Basically, if you help someone who was once in a situation similar to yours, you will feel better about yourself because you righted a wrong. You took a negative situation and made it positive; it's especially fulfilling if no one took the time to help you out. You are able to right the wrong of someone else and make someone else feel better.

How to improve your spiritual growth and feel better about yourself at the same time

When it comes to self esteem, you need to have a sense of right and wrong. How do you know what's right and wrong? We have laws that tell us, we have standards that define both right and wrong, and we have religion. When it comes to religion or spiritual power you have a sense of morally right or morally wrong standards. Everyone thinks that religion is about praying to a high god, but it also is about yourself and growing. Religion allows you to find comfort and strength to do what it is that you have to do. If you can find faith in anything, you will feel better about yourself.

Even if your faith is not in a God, but in yourself and your family; you can have spiritual growth without trying to find yourself in a religion. Spiritual growth is when you realize that there are things that you can control and things that you cannot. Spiritual growth is when you live for another person or spirit. If you live to serve God, you will feel better about yourself because there is power in the Bible. If you live to protect your child, you will feel better about yourself because you are sacrificing yourself for another. That is the basis of spiritual growth; living for something other than yourself.

How spiritual growth happens is something major has to happen to your life. You have to find a reason to live. You have to find something that gives you joy and that you are willing to go the distance for. Some people need a near death experience to have spiritual growth and some need things like a child to enter their life to finally get on the right path. That's how spiritual growth naturally processes, however, why wait for that. If you are non practitioner of a faith, find out why you stopped and then find out how to find yourself in faith. You need to support yourself, you need to believe in yourself, and you need to believe in something more than just yourself. Again, you need to find something to take up your devotion, not like a job, but it can be a person or it can be a spirit. The key to finding something to devote your time and energy is finding something that you would sacrifice everything for.

Religion is different for everyone; however it defines who you are and what you want out of life. It also helps you find the right path.

Regardless of your religion you will put your goals and ideas into a statement that is influenced by your religion. Then when you fail at a goal, you have your faith to fall back on. Your faith is what allows you to reach for better things. Your faith is what allows you to be a better person. You find strength and support in faith, regardless of what your faith may be.

For those who do not have faith in anyone or anything, you are lost and have a lot more than just personal growth to worry about. You still have to find yourself. Once you are able to find yourself and define who you are, then you will be able to grow by setting goals to be what it is that you want to be. For those who have no faith, finding faith is crucial to your living. You will never know what it feels like to help another person or you will never know what it feels like to be supported by others. If you can find faith or spiritual growth, then you will find personal growth.

How to be happier, personal fulfillment

To be happier and find personal fulfillment you have to be considered with two things. Those two things are honesty and faith. You need faith to be honest and you need honesty to have faith. The two tend to go hand in hand, however, if you can be true to yourself and be less selfish through faith, then you should have no problem feeling fulfillment in life. Most people say that to be happy you need to love much, laugh much, and live much. When it comes to the love, you need to be able to receive and to give love.

If you never feel what it is like to be loved, then you will never feel whole, like wise if you cannot give love. You need love in your life to feel complete. You should also find many things in your life to enjoy. You need to have people around you who can support you and share a laugh every now and then with. You need to define what makes you feel good about yourself and then seek those out.

Finally, you need to live much. Living is not just breathing, living happens to be much more than the basics. You need to see the world through other people's eyes. You need to take risks sometimes, but you also need to play it safe every now and then. You need to find the balance between the two. You cannot allow yourself to be held back by fear, but you must also learn to trust your instincts.

To feel fulfilled, you will need to make a list of everything that you would like to do before you die. Then place everything that seems important at the top of that list. Everyone's list should be different and you should never show anyone you list because they will discourage you with judgment. Once you have the list you need to take more steps towards achieving those goals. Every time that you reach a goal, mark it off and place a new goal on the list. This way you are constantly reaching out for new experiences. At one point in your life, if you have the three most important things on your list done, you can sit back and feel completed. You have done everything that you could possible want in life and more. You have succeeded!

The hardest triumph for a person is to feel self actualization or complete. In Maslow's hierarchy of needs there are five steps or basis needs for a person. One is your basic needs. You will always have shelter, food, clothing, love, and more, however you need to focus on the other four steps so that you can get to self actualization.

You need to focus on your safety, your self esteem levels, and social levels. To be fulfilled you have to satisfy your basic needs to live and then you have to satisfy your safety. When it comes to safety you will need to feel secure in your career, in your relationships, and in your finances. Once you can completely secured, you will then need to work on your social needs. You will need to build relationships with your family, friends, and co-workers. You need to be able to belong to a place. You need to feel like you are wanted at work, at home, and then your social circle. You will then need to work on your self esteem. Why do you feel the way that you do.

Once you have worked on your self esteem and become satisfied with you who are now, you can reflect on the other stages. Sometimes you are going to have repair the way you feel about the other stages, but once you have become content with your home, your personal life, social life, finances, and so on, you have become content and that is what self actualization is.

CHAPTER 4- ACCEPT ONE'S SHORTCOMINGS AND DEVELOPING ONE'S PERSONALITY

Sports are used to increase personal growth because you learn so many lessons on the field or court. You need to learn how to work as a team, how to support others, how to feel supported by others, and how to accept winning/losing in a graceful way. It helps kids became more social and it also helps them build lasting relationships. As you grow, you take those lessons and you learn from it. It also teaches you the difference between listening and hearing.

For those who do not know, hearing is the act of picking up vibrations and turning them into sound bites. Listening happens to be where you can comprehend those messages into phrases and sentences. You get the message, sort of speak. You not only hear someone talking, but you are listening to them and following directions. When it comes to sports, you have to know when to listen to someone and when you should listen to yourself. You need to learn when to follow instructions and when to give instructions. The key to sports is that it makes you a good leader. A good leader knows when to speak and when to listen. They know when to get ideas from teammates and when they need to give their team direction. You grow from sports because it teaches you how to be a good leader. If aren't a good leader, you lose. After a couple loses, you see what it takes to bring the team to victory. Also, when you are part of a team you get to know different people. It also teaches you how to deal with certain people.

If you look at Maslow's hierarchy of needs you have basic needs, safety, social, self esteem, and self actualization. When it comes to sports, you satisfy your basic needs by having a team. You get the attention and time needed to become a good athlete. You also get guidance needed to play the sport. Then for safety, you are taught how to play the game safely. You may also feel safe in a group to tell others how you feel and come up with your own ideas. There are so many people in a board room who do not speak because they are afraid to be judged.

They don't recommend good ideas because they are afraid. Sports teach you how to let people know your ideas regardless of being judged. It helps you feel comfortable speaking up. Then for social needs, sports allow you to feel like you are a part of something. It makes you feel important because you have a role and you need several other people to help you and there are several other people who are relying on you. Sport teams are a support system. If you get use to being part of a support system you won't feel so awkward in new situations and you will also understand you role in the group easier.

Teams also help with self esteem. Self esteem is the most important aspect of the hierarchy. If you don't have self esteem then you can never make it in the world and have fulfillment.

Sports give you self esteem so that you can be secured with who you are. You need to find a way that will make you feel good about yourself and sports is the ticket.

When you win in sports you feel so good about yourself, but if you lose, it can be a little hard to accept. It's the same way when it comes to goal setting. You will be able to set your goals and then if you fail, from being in sports, you will know how to pick up and accept your defeat, but still reach for better things.

How to make more friends

Do you feel some frustration because you think you don't have a lot of friends? It can be harder for some people to make friends. Some people have a personality that attracts people to them and they seem really popular, but even the popular ones worry about who is truly their friend. When it comes to friends, you shouldn't worry about the number. You should worry about how many of your associates would really be there to help bail you out of a jam. You should be considered with the people who you make friends with. You don't want to be friends with people who seem needy.

They have a certain behavior that might hinder you from having other friendships or even relationships. You know the saying, you can't choose your family, but you can pick your friends. When it comes to picking your friends you need to choose people worthy of your friendship. You don't want to associate yourself with people who have criminal behavior or who has serious issues with addictions.

If you are new to a place you will want to make your first connection, the right connection. If you are going to meet new people are you are going to have to go to spots that you would normally want to hang out and try striking up a conversation. You can start out with humor or you can start off with a "hello". If you strike up a conversation with someone who you have something in common with it is easier to keep the conversation going .Soon you can have a bond and then a friendship.

When it comes to places to meet new people, you can always start online. However, you need to make sure that you meet new people online in a safe way. Ask them to go out with you and a group of friends or co-workers. You can ask them to do things like bowling or shopping. The first thing though is to connect with the person. You will want them to be interested in some of the same stuff that you life, but they can still be unique and different from you. The only thing is that you don't want to meet friends online and then meet in person right away. You need to establish a bond before you allow new people in your life.

Once you have been hanging out with someone for awhile, you will want to make sure that you have a connection with them. You want to make sure that you feel secured in the friendship before you go into a best buds relationship. You will want to make sure that you choose your friends wisely. You don't want to have them running away when you really need them. You need to make sure that you know that they are going to stay with you when times get tough. If you are going to make friends, you might as well make lasting friendships.

Once you get older, making friends is harder. It's also harder to let friends go. If you are willing to make friends with a person, then you need to be sure that it's something that you want in your life. You don't want to be with a person who is needy, who constantly needs your approval, because no friendship should hinder you from having another. As you get older you want more support from friends, but it shouldn't be to the point where you are getting on their nerves. You need to make sure this is a friendship that you would want to pursue.

How to feel good even if you are away from home a lot

If you are someone that has to work away from your home a lot, you may find that you can get a little down once in a while. It may be a difficult situation when you find it necessary to do things outside the home, which means that you have to be away from your family and friends. It can be something that can be depressing at times and may even make you a little sad.

If you are looking for ways to feel good about yourself even if have to be out of the home a lot, you may want to try a few things. You need to find something that will make you feel better inside so that you are able to do the things that you have to. It may be your job that keeps you from your family most of the time. This is something that you cannot help and you will have to do if you want to support yourself and anyone else that depends on you.

If you are working outside of the home a lot, you may want to think about positive things that make you happy. When you are forced to work out side of the home, you may want to bring a long with you plenty of reminders that you have a great family waiting for when you return. You will want to have pictures, cards, and even tapes or CD's of your family and loved ones. This will help you to have comforting feelings with you so that you are not feeling so alone and depressed about being away from them for so long.

You should also make sure that you are taking the time to call anyone that you miss at home when you get the chance. Having a good cell phone plan, calling card or plenty of quarters is a great idea. You will want to call your family as often as you can so that you can hear their voice and talk to them about how you are feeling .you want to be able to share your feelings with them so that you can then feel better and be happy that you got to speak with them. This is a great way to lift up your spirits when you are not at home very often.

You should also make sure that you are spending as much quality time with your loved ones when you are home as you can. You want to make sure that you are getting to spend the amount of time that you want with them so that you can feel better about going away. You will want to make every moment count. You should make memories and make them last. You can take each of the moments with you and remember all the fun that you had with your loved ones when you are away from the house.

You should take the time to think about all the things that you want to do with your family when you get home as well. If you have a lot of quiet time or time to think, you should use this time to plan out what you can do with your family and friends when you get home .you can think of great ways to spend time with them and make the moments that you do have with them even more special. You will be glad that you did because you can take these moments with you and reflect on them when you are looking for something to make you smile.

It is hard to be away from your family all the time. You may find that you need to have some pick me ups from time to time. You should be prepared to have these feelings and you must be able to handle them. You want to make sure that you are not putting yourself at any danger of getting down in the dumps when you have to be away from home so much. Think good thoughts and remember that you will make up for lost time when you get home.

How to have personal fulfillment and a fulltime job

It can be hard when you have to work a full time job to make the ends meet. You may not want to be working all the time, but in today's society, we have to make sacrifices so that we can have a better life for our family and ourselves. We need to make the necessary changes in our life so that we can be happy and thrive with the financial situation that we have and be thankful that we have what we do. However, it can get depressing at times and we have to find a way to live a fulfilled life and be happy.

There are many things in this world that can bring us down. We have to make sure that we have all the things that we need in life so that we can be happy and satisfied when we can. We want to make sure that we are living each day to the fullest potential and you should never take anything for granted. It is not easy to do, but we do have to try so that we can make the most of each moment that we have.

If you have to work all the time, you may find that you are regretting some of your choices. You may find that you want to spend more time with your family and friends. It can be hard when you have to leave them behind all the time especially if you have children that you are missing important things with. You want to make sure that you are doing your best to make all the important events with your children that you can. You will find that they grow up fast and you do not want to miss anything that you cannot get back.

You will want to take the time off where your family and children are concerned. You will see that life passes by very fast and if you do not stop to enjoy the greatest things in your life; you will sadly regret them later on. You will want to try and make the most of your life and by spending quality time with those that you love, you will be better fulfilled and a happier person for it.

On your days off from work, you will probably have to do some chores and other things that you have to do. However, you should also fit in the things that you want to do. You may have hobbies and fun things that you really enjoy. If you are not doing them as often as you would like, you should take out time and do them. You may have to just forget the boring things like chores and housework and go out there and enjoy your life.

If you are always working and not having any fun, you will find that it will be a mistake on your part. You will not be happy and you may even find that you end up a little depressed. It can be difficult to go through life and not do anything that makes you happy. It is so very important to find something that you can do in your spare time that will fulfill you and give you the joy that you deserve. This will break you away from the tension and the stress that you may have if you are working a full time job.

Every now and then you have to break lose. You should not work all the time and not have anything to show for it. If you really want to have something, you should find a way to go out and get it. You will want to make sure that you are putting all your resources together to really get something that you have always wanted. This will make you happier and give you the feeling that you are working for more than just paying bills. You will feel that you have accomplished something and you will be fulfilling something that you want in your life.

How to feel good about yourself as a single parent

It can be very hard being a single parent. There are so many people out there that have to do this hard job on their own. Many men and women are living every day as a single parent and making the most of what they have. They want to raise great children and at the same time, they want to find something that makes them feel good about themselves. This is not always easy and may also take a little time to achieve as well.

You will want to do a few things so that you can continue to raise your children the way that you want to and also have a little bit of sanity at the same time. You need to stay balanced so that you can achieve all your goals and do the things in life that you want. You will want to pay attention and do what works for you and your family.

You should talk to your children and make sure that you are finding out what is going on in their life. You want to be sure they are happy and healthy and that they are making good choices. This is something that will boost your spirits and make you feel better about being a single parent. You will learn that you are doing your job and that you are good at it.

You should also make sure that you have support. You want to get whomever you can to make you feel that you have a sense of backup. You can use your family, friends or church to help you do this. You want to have good resources so that you can find strength and power to take on the rough things that happen in life. You want to be ready for these challenges so that you can make your goals and dreams come true for you and your family.

Always remember to take time out for you and your family. You should find ways to spend quality time together and to have fun. You want to make every moment count with your loved ones and your children especially if you are a single parent. You should make sure that you are giving each child one on one time as well as doing things as a family. This will give you the feeling that you are united together as you should be. You should also take time out for yourself from time to time. You need to get a break so that you can continue to have the sanity that you need to be happy. You should allow yourself the time to make friends outside the home so that you can have your own space as well.

Make sure that you have a daily routine. You want to have a good schedule and structure for you and your children. You will want to have chores set up for everyone as well as meal times and bedtimes set for certain timeslots. You want to keep these times and make your children stick to the rules. This will make it easier to enforce these rules and to give them structure that you know they need.

Find a good method of discipline. You want to be able to correct your children when it is necessary in the right manner. You want to talk to them in a way that they can understand what is right and what is wrong.

This is the best way to give them the values and the manners that are needed to have a good life. You want to enforce any rules that you set in the home so that you can keep a well-balanced life for the children and this will help you stay stabilized as well. You will not want to cave in and bend the rules just because you are asked. You will depend on this type of structure so that you can help control your children as you see fit. This will also make you feel good about raising well-behaved and responsible children.

Chapter 5- Personality Growth Needs Daily Workout

It is not always easy understanding and figuring out what we have to do in life to be a good person. It is sometimes hard to find out what we want to do in order to grow and be the person that we want to be. We have to figure out what is best for our life and go on from there. Everyone is different and there is usually no right or wrong answer to the question. It is all about growth and psychology and what it can do for us.

There are so many different books out there that try and teach us how to grow as a person and how to act. However, these books are not always a good help to everyone. There are many things in life that we have to consider and some of them may not be in any textbooks. We may have many other things going on in our life that we have to deal with and sometimes, they may be hard to deal with on our own.

In order for us to grow as people, we have to be willing to accept the things that are going on in our life. We have to find a way to understand what we are doing and what we want to be doing in our life. We may have to find a way to do the things that are important to us and that we have always dreamed about doing. It is not always easy, but we must find the psychology that will help us move on.

You can search through many different books and talk to therapists about what you should do or what they think you should do. However, you are the only person that can truly change your life. You are in complete control of your own destiny and you will want to be prepared for the things that come your way. You want to be the one that makes things happen for yourself and you will feel better knowing that you did what you could to make your life better.

You may have to go through some methods of psychology before you find the ways that work best for you. It may take some time, but you will see that there are different things that you can do to make the difference in your life. You will see that you will have many choices to make and you may even have to make sacrifices but in the end, you will feel better about who you are and what you were willing to do to make your life better. You will see that you will have many options and you are the only one that is in control of your destiny.

Take the time to think about how you want to grow as a person. You should think about the changes in your life that you think are necessary to achieve this goal. You will want to be sure about who you want to be and think about how you need to go about doing this. You will see that you can make a difference in your own life and do what makes you happy. This is the best way to make your life better and to become the person that you want to be. You may find that it is not always easy at first, but with some work and effort, you will have the strength to become the person in life that you want to become. Think about how you can make this goal happen for you.

Personal growth and aging, how to feel better about getting older

No one wants to grow older. It can be a sign of our own mortality. It is not always easy for everyone to take on the effects of getting older and what will happen as the result of it. We must find the strength to move on and go on through life the way that we want to. We need to make the right choices so that we can have got older and still be happy.

We have to be able to grow as adults and move on through life as we get older. This is a healthy way of accepting what we cannot change. There are ways that we have to grow and use the lessons that we learn from life to achieve goals and to become the person that we want to be. We have to find ways to feel good about who we are and what is happening to our body.

We need to find ways to feel good about who we are and what is going on throughout our life. We have to be able to find ways to be happy with who we are and what we are all about. We can choose to do things that will work best for us and that will make us happy and healthy. We may not be able to beat getting older, but we sure can fight it as much as we can. We can use out best ability to make ourselves become who we want to be.

Exercise is one way that we can help fight aging. We can do exercises that work best for us. There are things that we can do that will get our heart pumping and also make us feel great. Walking, running, swimming and any other outdoor exercise is a great way to get in shape and to also feel good from the inside out.

Mr. and Mrs. Personality
We can enjoy the great outdoors while also getting in shape and feeling great about who we are and what we are doing.

When we move our bodies and get in motion, we are fighting off the act of aging and getting our minds and bodies in shape. When we feel healthy physically, we are putting our emotional well being in good shape as well. This is something that we all need to do so that we can be well balanced and able to take on the challenges of everyday life.

Finding out what you can do for your life is something that you can do to make you grow as a person too. You can try new things and get introduced to fun and excitement. This is something that will keep you healthy and feeling young. When you are trying new things, you will see that you are able to enjoy more than just the same old things that you once did. There is no sense in staying bored and unhealthy, you will find that when you are able to keep motivated in life, you are going to feel better and be able to feel good about yourself and your body as well.

There is no sense in not being happy in this world just because you are getting older. We all have to do it. The best thing that you can do is making the most of each day and lives life to the fullest. When you are able to look back on the great memories that you had, you will feel good about your life. You do not want to waste one minute in life. Having a life full of "I wish I did that" or any type of regret is only going to bring you down. This is not the way that you want your life to be. You want to be glad that you had the opportunities that you had so that you are able to have great memories and feel good about reflecting back on your life.

How to find personal growth through exercise

Exercise is something that you can do for yourself that will make you feel good. You want to make sure that you are doing the best that you can with what you have. You should not sit back and just take life as it comes. You want to do the things in life that you want so that you are able to look back on your life and feel great. One way to do this is to find the right exercise that works best for you.

Exercise is one of the best ways to feel good. You want to feel great from the inside out. There is nothing better than being happy and healthy at the same time. When you have the right method of exercise, you will see that you can put your life on the right track and get your heart pumping. Taking the time to put your health first is very important. When you are able to grow as a person and use exercise as a method of release, you will feel good about who you are.

Getting out to do exercise is a good idea. You can join a gym to get out there and get motivated. Sometimes exercising at home is not always the best method for everyone. There are many people that need the extra push to get them on the right track. You can get involved with many of the local organizations and join a health club that will put your needs first. This is a great idea that will help you strengthen your body and feel better about who you are and your personal growth.

If you are someone that can exercise from your home and stay motivated, you should do it. You can buy some extra gym pieces that you think will help you achieve your personal goals. You can get anything that you want or like to help you get in shape. You will see that once you start a good exercise routine, you will want to stay motivated and on track. This will get you the results that you want so that you can feel good about growing as a person.

Another way to exercise is to get outside and do what you want. You can play sports or take up a great hobby outside. You will enjoy getting out there and getting great exercise as well as getting fresh air that will help to get the blood pumping. This is one way to feel great about you and to be able to make your body work hard at staying in shape. You will want to keep in shape so that you are able to look and feel your best. Working hard is going to take some time, but eventually you will see that you can adapt to getting in shape and this will make you a better person.

Personal growth is something that you want to feel good about. You will want to make sure that you are proud of who you are and what you are achieving in life. You will want to do something that will grab your attention. You can join a club, find a great hobby or meet some new friends that will help you make your life better. This is going to be a great idea that will keep you feeling as good as you can. You will appreciate this when you see what a better person it makes you and how you start to feel about yourself.

How to find personal growth through your children

We all have to find a way to grow as a person. This is something that is not always easy. You may have to find a resource that will make it easier for you to find out who you are and what you want to be in life. This is going to take a little bit of time, but there are things that can help us find out whom we are and what we want to do in life. We can actually grow through our children. Children can help us find out who we want to become and what we want from life.

There are things that we are not sure of in life. However, when we have the right help, we can find out anything that we want. We can grow into the people that we are destined to become as we take on the challenge of helping our children to become great adults.

We will see the way that life can affect what and us we need to do in order to be a better person and live, as we want to.

As much as we teach our children, they will actually teach us great lessons as well. They will show us things that we never knew before. We will see life through their eyes if we just allow ourselves to think about it. We can walk in their shoes and see what life has for us out there. All we need to do is keep an open mind and let our children teach us what they know. This is a great way for our personal growth be discovered and move on to bigger and better things in life.

There is nothing better in life than raising great children. We want to do the best that we can so that we can feel proud about who they have become. We want to try and instill the best possible manners that we can in our children. This will make them become the great adults that we know they can become. When we see them growing each day and doing the things that make them happy as well as doing great things for others, this will make us feel good inside.

We can also enjoy the great life that they are living. We can walk through life with them and make each moment last. We want to make memories with our children so that we can use them to reflect on later in life. This is something that will comfort us later on and make us happy. We want to be able to remember all the great things that we experienced with our children and make sure that we use these moments to help make us grow as people.

The best thing that you can do for yourself and your child is to communicate with them. You want to be able to talk to them about anything. The more comfortable that they feel with you means that the more they will open up to you about anything. You can have open and honest relationships that will eventually help both of you grow. You can become stronger and happier just by having each other to lean on. This is something that everyone needs in their life so that they can become better adults and have the life that they know they deserve. You can grow into the person that you want as well as watching them become the person they want to become too. You can both grow together and fulfill your dreams and goals as life goes on.

Personal growth and your home, making your house a home

Growing as a person is very important. You want to do this in your own home. It is important to feel like you are at home and comfortable when you are in your house. You want to feel safe and secure because this is the one place where you can go to be yourself. You want to have the feelings of security and serenity each time you enter your home. Personal growth is something that you can achieve when you are making your house your home.

You want to be open minded when you are thinking about your home. You want to think about what will make you comfortable and what you like. You should incorporate all the things that you like the most so that you are truly making this your very own space. You want to put a little bit of your personality and your own creativity into your home. This is what makes it so very special.

You want to feel like you can do anything and be anyone when you are in your home. This is the one place that you do not have to think about what you do first. You are in complete control and you have the opportunity to make the house that you reside in the one retreat that you can feel your best at all times. You want to make sure that others feel as good as you do too.

When you are bringing joy to your home, you will see that you will have a positive experience and one that you will enjoy. You will want to make sure that you are filling your home with things that make you feel good about who you are and what your needs are. You should listen to your inner being and think about what makes you happy. Once you have these things, you can then bring them into your home and make it what you feel good about.

Taking the time to think about what you want for your home is not always easy. You may not know what will make you feel the most comfortable in and you may need to take some time to think about how you can make your house a home. When you are sure of what you want in your life, you can use these ideas for your home. You want to be able to come home to a place that is all your own and that you can relax in and feel your best.

Remember that one of the things you should be thinking about when you are trying to make your house a home is that you need to make others feel good. You want to make your home as inviting and as warm as you can. You want your guests to feel like they are welcome each time they enter your door. This is one way that you are ensuring that your house is defiantly a home. You can appreciate the feeling that you get each time you see someone feel at ease when they come to your home. It will make you feel better knowing that you are growing as a person and that these things are important to you.

You do not have to put a lot of money into making your house a home. You do not have to fill it with things; you need to fill it with love. This is one of the most important things that you can give to your house to make it a home. You want to use your feelings and your personality to fill your home with the things that make you feel better about who you are and being home.

Personal growth and development, it starts as a child

The way that you think and act will start when you are a child. You will learn things from a very early age. You will find out what you like and dislike and you will also start to develop your personality. When you are a child, this is a very precious time and one that wills you will want to remember for as long as you can.

You will start to become who you are meant to be when you are a child. You will learn how to be a good person and how to make your life what you want it to be. There are many influences in your life as a child. There will be your family and your friends and you see many different ways to act and live. Sometimes you may pick up on these influences and it may cause you to act a certain way. It is important to keep in mind what you want to do in life so that you are able to pick the right influences in your life.

When you are a child, there will be many people in your life. You will have your parents, siblings, family, teachers and so many more. Many times, you can get confused about what you are supposed to be doing and how you should act. It can be very difficult when it comes time to figuring out what you want to be in life and how you should be acting. Growing up is one thing that you need to take in slowly so that you can remember each moment that you have.

Getting to be the adult that you want to be is very important. You may have to make sacrifices and change the way you look at life. It is not always easy to get to where you need to go. You may find that it is a bit difficult finding out what you want to be but you can achieve your personal and your emotional goals. There is no reason why you should have to be one certain way. You have the right to make your own choices and to think about how you want to act as a person. There is nothing better than feeling great about which you have become in life.

When you are growing up from childhood, you will learn that there are things that you need to do and things that you should not do. You need to make sure that you are able to determine the difference between good and bad. You will find that you have to make choices for what you think will make your life better and make you a better person. You will want to make your choices wisely because what you decide as a child will affect how you grow into an adult.

It will depend on how you grow up and your atmosphere. You need to make sure that you are in a good environment and that you have the best possible life. Sometimes there are things that you cannot control. If you are in a bad situation that you cannot control as a child, there is nothing that you can do about that. However, you will learn different life lessons and this will teach you how to be a better person. You will see how you can self improve your life and the way that you think.

You can remember things that you will learn as you are growing up as a child. There are many lessons out there for you and you have to be willing to take each opportunity that you have and use it towards your own self-growth.

Personal growth and fulfillment, teaching your child about self-esteem

Self-esteem is one thing that you have to have .you need to feel good about yourself and who you are. You need to make sure that you are putting these good self esteem habits into your children as well. You need to give them the feelings from the time they are born that they are worth something and that they deserve to have only the very best in life. This is something that will stay with them for a lifetime.

Mr. and Mrs. Personality

You need to start from the time the child is born. You will want to make sure that you are able to give them the power that they need from the beginning so that they can feel good about themselves. You want to be able to teach a child the right and the wrong way to do things as well. The better you teach your child, the better they will grow up and be better people as adults.

Give your children the learning experiences that they need from the beginning. You want to teach them life lessons that will help them make better choices. You need to make sure that you allow them to also grow, as they need to. You will not want to make them feel bad about who they are because this is the way that they will learn how to do things in life. Self-esteem is something that is learned and instilled into children. You need to make them feel good about who they are and what they do in life.

You do not want to give your child the feeling that they are better than everyone else. This is only going to make life harder for them as they go on. You will not want to give them the feelings that they deserve more than what other people do. You want them to have respect for others and take other people's feelings into consideration. You will want to make sure that you are able to show them that they have to appreciate others too. You need to show them that you need to be respectful of how others feel and what they think. This will make them better people.

Giving your children the ability to make good choices on their own will allow them the power to make good choices. You will see that they will feel better about who they are and what they are doing. This is a great way to make an impact on any child's life. You want them to feel good about who they are and what they are doing in life. You will want to make sure that you are able to give this to your child so that you can raise them to have plenty of self-esteem.

If you are not sure about how to give your child more self esteem, you should think about how you get yours. Think about ways that you can make these situations move on to them. You want your child to have the same good feelings in life that you have. You will want to be able to give them all the strength and the power they need to make good choices for their life and to give them many great opportunities for the road that lies ahead of them.

You can get a sense of accomplishment when you are helping your child develop good self-esteem. Having low self-esteem can make it very difficult for anyone to get to where they want to be in life. Achieving goals are very important. Without the right tools and the sense to go after it, you will find that many dreams are let down and self-esteem problems will come apparent. You want to bring their self-esteem levels as high as you can for a great childhood and even into adulthood.

Chapter 6- Great Tips to Love Your Personality

In order to feel good about yourself, you want to learn how to be yourself. You have to realize that you do not have to change who you are and what you do in life. You can be a good person and learn to feel comfortable with who you are and what you are doing in life. You need to find a way to let your inner being out so that others can get to know you too.

There are many people that are afraid to just be themselves. This does not have to be the case. You can learn how to show off your inner personality and you will find that others will like whom you are and what you are about. You should not feel self-conscious about who you are inside. You may surprise yourself and find that people do not care about the superficial stuff. They just want to learn who you are and get to know the real you.

Finding out how to be you around others may take some time. You may not be able to do this all at once. You may find that it takes a bit of work. You will first want to think about how you can let others get to know you. You want to go out and make friends. You should not hide the real you because you will feel like it is all an act each time you meet up with them. You want to be yourself and let others see who you are. Get it out of the way first thing. Otherwise, you may find that you are exhausted trying to hide the real you and what you stand for.

Getting out there and learning to be comfortable with who you are may take some getting used to. You want to first start out small and work your way up to showing your true inner side. You should not be ashamed about who you are and how you feel about certain things. Remember that your opinion counts too. You are special and important. Why wouldn't you want to show that off? You need to feel good about yourself. This is all part of good self-esteem and confidence that you have in yourself.

Do not let others get to you? Remember that of course not everyone in life is going to like you. There will be people out there that your personality will clash with. However, this is not reason to get discouraged. You need to express yourself and if someone cannot handle that, this is his or her problem. You should only surround yourself with people that make you feel good about yourself. Being around the other downers will only put a damper on your personality too.

The only way to live a happy life is if you are honest about who you are and what you want in life. It is not that hard to find out how to do this. With a little self-respect and some dignity, you will see that you can make your own life as special as it can be. You will be glad that you took the time to make these dreams happen and go on from there. You will feel good about how you are standing up for yourself and making others know that you do feel like you are special and that you are worth a lot more.

Getting to feel like you can be yourself around everyone may take some time, but with some work, you will get there and once you do you will know that it is worth the effort.

Five methods of finding personal happiness in life

Happiness is not something that comes easy to all of us. It is something that we may have to work on. We have to find a way to learn to be happy regardless of anything that happens in our life. It is something that we can do and do well. We do not have to worry about what others think, because this is our life and as far as it is known, we only get one chance in life and we have to make it great.

There are some methods that you can try so that you have all the happiness in life that you deserve. It is going to take some work and a lot of effort, but you can do it and once you see the way that you feel, you will know that it is worth it and that you have made the right choices in life. Taking these methods into consideration is very important. You need to make things work for you so that you are able to do well in life and to get all your goals achieved.

Without happiness, life is meaningless. We have to first set goals. Once we have goals in place and we know what we want, we have to figure out a way to get there. We need to find ways to make things happen for us so that we can have the very best in life that we deserve. We need to make our life special so that we are able to feel good at the end of the day. When we are setting goals that we want in life, we will be able to start to feel good about our life because we will have a goal to work hard for.

Second, we need to remember that we have to live for today. We need to make sure that we are using our best intentions and making the days that we have worthwhile. We need to of course think about our future and make sure that we are making the right choices so that we are safe and secure, but we also need to bring some fun to our life and to make sure that are succeeding in all our goals.

Another thought is to think about what would make us lose our happiness. What could happen in our lifetime that would make us feel badly about who we are and not be happy anymore? These are things that we defiantly need to stay away from. We have to make sure that we are able to keep the negative things out of our life so that we are able to make good choices without risking looking our happiness. We need to make sure that we are able to make these things work for us and to continue to stay happy.

Being healthy is the fourth thing that we need to do to ensure that we are happy. We need to make good health choices so that we are able to stay happy and healthy no matter what we do. We need to continue to eat the right way and to think about the choices that we make for our body. We need to keep ourselves from anything that will make us unhealthy and sick. We have to keep the negative things out of our body and also stay in good mental health so that we are able to be emotionally and physically happy as well.

Lastly we need to keep the good feelings in our hearts. We have to be able to keep these good feelings in our mind so that we can give back to others. We need to be pleasant and to try and be happy. The more pleasant that we are will mean that we will be able to stay happier as well as make others happy too. We want to make other people feel good about them. We want to be able to bring joy to others and keep thinking good thoughts. Do not let yourself get down and especially do not intentionally bring others down.

Five methods of finding more in life, with your family, personal growth

We all want more out of life. However, we need to realize that it is not just going to jump up and grab us. We have to make things happen in our life. We need to keep pushing ahead and get to where we want to be. There are many obstacles that will try and push us back. When this is the case, we need to stay on top of the game and get to where we want to be. It can happen and it will.

There are five things that we can do to find more in life. We can do this with our family and our own personal growth as well. All we have to do is be willing and open to go out there and do the work. Once we figure out what we want from our life, we can then go out and start making things happen. This is something that can work for us and even for our family and friends as well.

You should think about what you want to do in your life. Think about the goals and the dreams that you have set for yourself. When you think about the things that you want to accomplish you should use this as finding more in life. You need to push ahead of the game and go out there in search of the life that you have in mind. When you figure out what you want to do in life, you will be happier and more fulfilled.

Next you need to make sure that you are willing to explore with your family. Take the time to learn about who your family is and what they need from you. You want to do this if you have children and spouses too. You will see that you can become closer to them just by finding out more about who they are and what they want in life. You will have a better relationship with them and you will see that you can communicate better when you know how they are feeling and what they are looking for in life. This is a great way to find out more about your life and what you need.

Take time to have fun. When you are ready to get out and take a break you will see that you will be able to get out and enjoy life and all that it has for you to take in. you can get caught up in the daily rush of life and everyone needs to take some time for themselves. You need to find something that you like and go out there and take in the fun. You will be able to find out more about yourself and get rid of the added stress that bothers you.

You need to find out where you are spiritually too. If you are not sure what you believe in or what you need to do for this, you should take the time to research the subject. Think about what your spiritual side is and what you want it to become. When you are sure that you are able to feel good about who you are in this area, you will feel more secure and more stable. You will feel better inside and this will reflect on the outside too. You will find yourself through your spiritual side too.

Be willing and open to trying new things. When you are stuck with the same old things, you will find that you may get stuck in a rut. You may find it hard to move on to new and interesting things; however this is the only way that you will find out more about who you are and what you like. You will get to try new things and this will get you to find out more about your own life and the way that you feel. You should take the opportunity when they come up to get interested in new things. Take time and at least try them. If you do not like it, you can always find something else. You will be surprised at how much you can learn from different opportunities and how it will help you grow as a person.

Five methods of finding personal success and growth in reading

You will be amazed at what you can learn through reading. You will see that there are so many things that you can do in your life with the right knowledge. When you are ready to start succeeding in life, you should take the time to read. This is an amazing thing and you will see how it can work for you.

There are many ideas that you can get through reading. You will be greatly amazed at the opportunities that you can come up with when you simply take the time to read and make the most of your life. You will be able to find out so many different things and you will be able to take advantage of the opportunities that are out there for you. Get started now and read your way to success.

First, you should read about things that interest you. If you are having an interest in something and you want to learn more about it, you should take the time to read. You can learn all the things that you were wondering about and so much more. There are so many books out there that have information about everything. You can even go online and find out what you are looking for. There are many opportunities that you can open up when you have the right information.

Second if you are looking for a way to make yourself more successful, you should take the time to find out what you need to do in order to get to where you want to be. You can do this by reading. Reading is a great way to get the facts about what you need to make your life better and what you can do to get yourself there.

Third of all, you can need to use reading as a way to make yourself smarter. Just by reading books, you are using your mind. You will see that no matter what you are reading, you are putting information into your brain. This is something that is very useful. You are getting your mind working and putting it to good use. You should take this opportunity any time that you can. You will feel good when you know that you are helping yourself succeed just by reading books.

The fourth way that you can use reading to help you find success is that you can help others. When you are reading, you can use this as a good method of helping others. You can read about anything and then you can use what you have learned and spread it on. You can show others how they too can learn to be successful by reading. You are doing not only yourself a favor, but you are helping others as well. This is a great feeling and one that you should be proud of.

The fifth method of making yourself more successful by reading is to use this as power. When you are giving yourself the power to read about anything, you are giving your mind and body more strength. You are putting yourself ahead of the game and giving yourself so much opportunity. You are getting all the advantages of reading and the power that it has. This is a great goal and one that you need to take advantage of anytime you get the opportunity to.

Reading is a great tool to use. You will find that reading is something that you will use forever. No matter what you are doing and what you need, reading is one way to get you there. You cannot go wrong no matter what you decide to read. You are opening up your mind and letting yourself take in power by giving it knowledge.

Five methods of personal growth in the arts

You can learn so much just by letting yourself see all the different things that are in the world. You will want to put yourself in front of all the opportunities that you can find. Letting yourself grow, as a person with the arts is something that you will find useful. You can get to use this information as a great learning experience for life and the things that you want out of it.

Mr. and Mrs. Personality

You can first of all use art to help you find out more about yourself. You should take some time out to explore the things that you like. You can go out and check out all the different pieces of artwork that are out there. You will take some interest in some of the arts and other pieces will not be your taste. However this is a great way to find out what you like.

The second method of personal growth in the arts is to use it for entertainment purposes. You will be able to use these things as a great way to express who you are and what you want others to see about yourself. You can decorate your home and express the way that you feel through art. This is something that a lot of people do. You will be surprised at the reaction that you will get from many people.

Third of all, you may want to use your interest in art to help see the world. You can explore great places when you are willing to travel. You will be amazed at all the wonders of the world that you can come in contact with when you are using art as way for personal growth. You will be opening up your mind and using this great experience as something that will help you find out more about who you are and even what you want in life.

The fourth method of using the arts to help personal growth is by using it to as your career. If you are someone that really has an interest in what art has to offer, you can use this experience as something that will take you ahead in the art business. You can have a great amount of success when you use art as your major. You will learn about the financial part as well as the fun and entertainment that you will get from this type of career. It is something that you should think about if you love art and want to see what it can offer you.

The last thing that you can do to improve your life with the arts is to learn to appreciate it. You will see that you can learn a lot from checking out the arts. You can widen your environment and get to see different things that you never would have dreamed about. You will see that there are many great features that you can learn about from art. Getting to see the world through the eyes of art is a great way to get to where you want to be. Art is an amazing thing and you should learn to stop and check it out when you can.

Five methods of personal growth involving traveling

Seeing the world is a great way to get to where you want to be. You should think about the things that you want and how you can learn from them. You may want to think about traveling for some great personal growth. You can get to where you want to be in life when you are willing to go the distance and make the most of what you have.

You should think about where you would like to go first of all. If there is a certain place that you have always wanted to be, you may want to think of how you can get there. This is something that can get you a great deal of knowledge and a lot of fun as well. You can travel to anywhere in the world. The only thing that can stop you is money. You may want to save up your money until you have enough to get you where you want to be. This will teach you to save for the things that you really want in life.

As you travel the second thing that you can learn is that you can see different parts of the world. You will see and get to learn about the different cultures that are going on around us. You can learn about how other communities live and see many other interesting things that you would not be able to see if you were to never leave your home. You should not be afraid to go out there and experience the world that is around you.

Mr. and Mrs. Personality
The third thing that you can learn from the world of travel is that you can experience fun. You should go out and have as much fun as you can. There is a huge world out there for you to experience and you should make the most of what you can. You will see that you can make a huge impact on your life just by going to different places and seeing the world that is around you.

Fourthly, you can learn personal growth by traveling and seeing what the big world has out there for you. You will be able to get closer to your family and friends by traveling with them. Taking great vacations and trips is a super way to get closer to anyone that you do not get to spend a great deal of time with. You will be able to take in all the fun and excitement that is out there for you. You will have so much fun and will be able to communicate with them without the bothersome things that you normally would in daily life.

The fifth thing that you can learn from travel is to go after the things that you love the most in life. You will see that if you work hard and use your good judgment you can achieve things in life that you want. You will be able to get to where you want to go and use your time as great learning experience for personal growth. You will grow as a person by letting yourself take in all that you do with your travels. You will want to work harder so that you can get to see more places in the world. You can get what you want in life if you are willing to sacrifice and get the things that you have always dreamed about your entire life.

Traveling is something that you can do anytime. You can go far distances or you can go shorter ones. No matter where you go, there is a lesson to learn and you should open your mind to these experiences and get to where you want to be in life. You will learn to appreciate these times and get more excited about the places that the future will hold for you.

Chapter 7- Moving On, Greatly Contributes your Personality

How to deal with growth and death, how to deal with a loss

Dealing with a death in your family is not always easy. It can be a very devastating time that you will have to learn to live with. You will need to find a way to go on and move past the hard times and accept what has happened. This may not always be easy, but you have to do it in order to move on and get on with your life.

Losses will happen to us from the time we are children. We have to learn how to deal with these problems and move past them. We will start this process early in life if we lose a pet or a favorite friend that moves away from us. This is a form of loss and will get us prepared for the downs in life. This will help us to take on the difficult challenges of the larger losses that will come in life later on.

Having to deal with a loss of a loved one is something that can bring traumatic stress on us. There are stages in which we have to move through the grief and these stages are going to help us find our way to get through what we have to do. The stages of loss are only described as what is best for you. You will see what you have to do for yourself to get back on track and to start feeling good again.

There are many articles and books out there for us to check out when we have a problem dealing with grief. It is not easy to move past this terrible time, but with the help of books and friends that have been through it before; we can learn how to use it for a learning experience. We want to move past the grief and start using this time as a way of improving our life and making each day count for something. We have to make sure that we are living life to the fullest and this is a great way to make sure that we do it.

If it is really hard to move on past the death of a loved one, the best choice for us may be to get counseling. This may be the only way that we are able to find out what we can do to make things right again. We may have to make the necessary changes in our life so that we are able to move on and get to where we need to go. Counseling can help us bring out our fears and our anger and find a way to deal with the pain that these things cause. These are very strong emotions that can be very difficult to deal with. It is something that we have to do in order to make this time pass a little bit easier.

If the death of your loved one is expected, it can be a little bit easier to deal with the loss. You may have had to watch them suffer for a period of time and this can be very painful. You may be glad to see them finally released of their agony so that they can move on to a better world and you can feel good that they are in a better place. This is something that you can almost look forward to.

You will not want them to suffer and by them dying, it will bring you some peace in your soul.

If the loved one dies unexpectedly like in an accident or because of a sudden illness, this can be very traumatic. It can almost in some cases, be very difficult to deal with and to face. You will want to block it out and not deal with any of the issues that you may have. This is not something that you can do. You need to bring yourself to understand what is going on and then find a way to deal with all the feelings that you have inside.

If you do not want to go to counseling, you should talk to a family member or friends that you feel comfortable with. You will want to get your feelings out in the open so that you are able to start the healing process. Once you have begun this process, you will see that you can get through the pain and move on to find happiness once again. You will always miss your loved ones, but you will feel better and realize that you have to go on and someday you will meet again.

How to find personal growth through your career

The way that we do our job is very important to us. We want to do it well so that we are able to make the most of our life and do what we need to in order to be great. We want to be proud of who we are and what we are doing. There are so many great things that we can accomplish through our life and doing something that we love is very important. You want to be able to make the most of your life and grow from the career choices that you make.

Having a great career is something that we all want. Not everyone gets to do for a living what they want. They may have to settle for a job that they are not so happy with because it pays the bills and gets them through life. This is not what we want in life, but in some cases, it is what we have to accept. It is not always easy to feel good about who we are when this is the case.

If you are looking for some type of personal growth through your career, you will want to make sure that you are able to be happy with what you are doing. You will want to make sure that you are giving your best so that you are able to achieve the goals and the dreams that you have always wanted. You want to be proud of who you are and what you are doing. Going to work each day with a smile is something that will make you grow into the person that you want to become.

When you are looking for something that will make you happy, you should turn to your career. You will want to make sure that you are doing something that makes you feel that you are doing what you were meant to do. You will want to do something with your life that is meaningful and exciting. This is the only way that you will be able to get to where you want to be with your own personal self.

There are many things that you can do to grow as a person through your career. You can learn how to be more professional and how to deal with the things in life that are sometimes not always easy. You will find that when you are able to things that make you feel good, you will be able to go home with a positive feeling. That is the most important thing that you can do for yourself. You want to be positive and keep the negative feelings out.

When you are looking for personal growth, you should be able to use your career for just that. You will need to be able to deal with things even if they do not go your way and how you expect them to. You want to be prepared for the bad and take the good with dignity. This is something that you will learn when you are doing the job in life that you love the most. There is nothing wrong with wanting to be great and when you have the drive and the determination in life to do it, you will get there.

Live out your dreams and do not accept anything but the best. You want to be someone that you can feel good about and you want the respect that you deserve from others. This is the only way that you will be able to grow in the way that you want to and move on to all your dreams and goals that you want. You can feel great about who you are and what you are doing when you have the will to do just that and so much more.

Personal growth and getting fired, how it can help you

No one wants to hear those terrible words; "you are fired!" they can be the hardest words to hear in life. However, hearing these words do not have to be the end of the world. They can actually be the beginning of a new life for you. You will find more opportunities and be able to achieve your goals even if you are not feeling so great right now. You will see that things will get better and all you have to do is be willing to take this chance.

You will want to go on and find your purpose in life. You will want to evaluate the situation and what is going on. You will want to take a look at your skills and qualifications. Think about what you can do and what you want to do with your life. Think of the possibilities and what you can achieve if you really go after it. This can be a great life changing experience if you let it happen for you.

You will want to also give yourself some time to adjust to the fact that you have been fired. This can be a traumatic time and you will want to think about how you are feeling and what you want to do about it. Be honest with yourself and your family about how you are feeling and what you want to do. You should not be afraid to ask them for help if you need it and to get support from them as well.

You will first want to update your resume. You should add anything that is new and exciting and put in your recent accomplishments. Make sure that you are creating the very best resume that you can so that you can grab the potential employee's attention and get the job that you are hoping for in the future.

You should also try and save money. You should not be going out and spending a lot if you have been recently fired. You want to find ways to save money in case you do not find a job right away. Put yourself on a budget and stick to it. You should make your minimum monthly payments on credit cards and get rid of the unnecessary debt or other expenses that may be coming your way. You need to think responsibly so that you are able to get through this time period and look forward to the next chapter in your life.

You can also use your being fired as some time that you can spend with your family. This may be the best way that you can get to catch up with them and find out what is going on. You can spend some quality time with your friends that you have not seen in a while. You should make some time for yourself and get to have some fun. If you have children, spend some time with them. Use this to your advantage and not as something that is so terrible. Invite old friends over for dinner or take in a movie with your spouse. These are great examples of what you can get achieve personally when you are fired from your job.

You may also want to think about going back to school. This is a great idea that will defiantly get you ahead of the game. This can be something that can move you ahead and put you where you want to be. You can go out there and get the degree that you have always wanted and put some great confidence in yourself again.

Be positive and put your feelings ahead of everything else. You want to be able to move past getting fired, but you also want to think of things that you can do to make this a learning experience and to give it some purpose. You will see that you can come out a winner and find personal strength and growth from this ordeal.

Chapter 8- Wear the Perfect Personality When You are Rearing

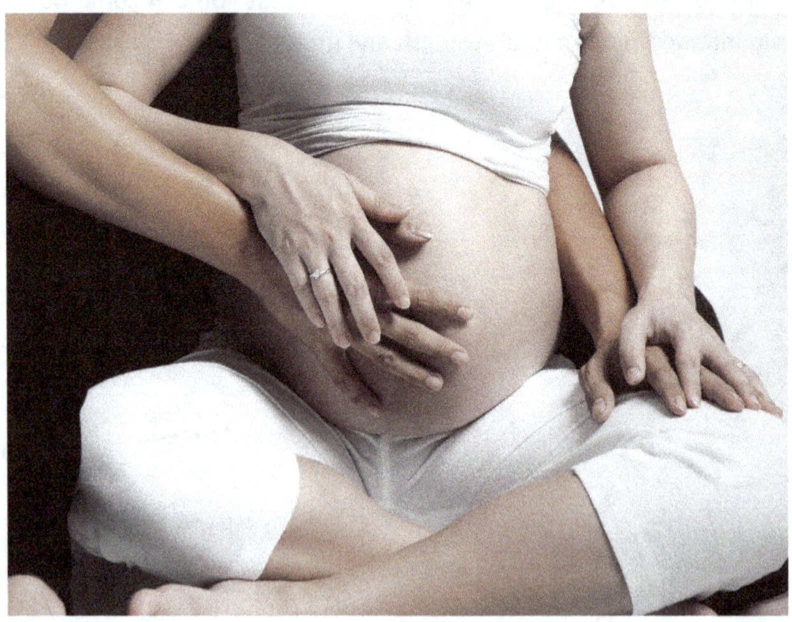

Five methods of personal growth while you are pregnant

When you are pregnant, it is not always easy. It can be a very joyous time as well as being very scary. A woman has many emotions running through her mind and she may have a lot of unanswered questions. This whole other person is growing inside their body and they are not sure what is going to happen. All they really know is that they are growing as a person and they will want to find the right methods to do this.

The first method of personal growth while you are pregnant is to feel great. You need to know that you are doing one of the most important jobs there is. That job is creating a life. This is a great and exciting thing that will make you feel incredible. It is very scary and even a little bit frustrating at times, however it is something that will make you realize what you are put on this great earth to do.

The second method is to understand how important life is. You may have not always realized what life was all about. You may have played hard and did a lot of things that you should not have done. However with the right choices now, you can make your life turn into something that you would not have expected. You can be great and you can accomplish great things once you have used this experience as a method of personal growth.

Thirdly, you can use this experience to figure out how special you are. You may be feeling a little bit down and depressed, however, there is no need to go out and have these feelings. You should be proud of the person that you are and that you are about to bring a great person into this world. You will find that you are doing something so amazing that it will change who you are and how you feel forever.

There is nothing better than getting to be the person that you want to become. The fourth method of personal growth while you are pregnant is that you will start to feel more responsible. You are not in control over two people in the world, you and the baby. You will want to learn how to make sure that you are there for the child now and after they are born for many years to come. You will have to grow up as a person and take charge of being a good parent. This is a difficult challenge, but one that you can succeed with.

The last method of personal growth when you are pregnant is to be independent. You are not always going to be able to depend on others to be there for you. You need to make sure that you are willing to take control over certain situations. When you are able to take care of yourself and make the right choices for your life, you will see that you are independent and that you can take care of yourself. This is something that will excite you and get you ready for all the challenges that lie ahead. It is a very scary time, but one that will make you the person that you know you want to become.

When you are willing to take these five methods of personal growth into consideration when you are pregnant, you will see what a difference it will make in your life and how you will be a better person from it.

Five methods of personal growth after children

Having children is a great experience in life. It is something that you need to make sure that you are ready for. You will have to be ready to take on the challenges of all that you need to do and so much more. You will want to make sure that you are doing the things that you need so that you are raising great children and also making time for yourself.

Children can teach you a lot and you will first want to pay attention to what they can teach you. You will be able to find out many new and creative things. Just by listening to your children, you can learn a lot about whom you are and what you want to do in your own personal life. You will find this a great way to get to where you want to be and so much more.

There are many different things that you can do to make your life better after children. You can find out that you were meant to be a parent. This may be the one thing that makes your life worthwhile. You will see that you can make your life better by listening to your child. You will want have fun with them and use this time as a great way to get closer to them.

Having fun after children is one thing that may change after having children. You may have to learn how to have a different kind of fun. You may not be able to have the same lifestyle that you once did. You can no longer go out and party like before. You will want to tone it down a little and stay at home more. Finding out what you can do with your children for fun is a great idea. You can have a lot of fun and entertainment just by playing with them and doing the things that they like.

You will learn a lot about yourself after having children. You will see that you are no longer the most important thing in the world anymore. You will want to make sure that you are taking the best possible care of your children that you can. You want to provide them with a good and stable home that they can feel safe and sound in. You will want to make sure that you are getting the things that they need as well as giving them a safe environment that they will be glad to grow up in.

Taking time to teach your children important values is something that you need to do as well. You will want to make sure that you are instilling in them something that you want them to take with them. This is the fifth method of personal growth. You can grow with your children and see what each day brings you. You may have to be a little patient and let life happen, but it is something that you will have to look forward to. This is an amazing time that you should appreciate and use as a learning experience for you and your child.

When you have the right methods of personal growth after children, you will be able to teach them things that you think are important and what you want them to think about. You will want to make the most of this experience and value each and every moment. You will want to be sure that you are comfortable with the things that you do to help your child grow. Make sure that you make memories with your children and use them to reflect on years on down the road when you want to remember the great times.

How to find personal growth with a family

Mr. and Mrs. Personality

There are plenty of ways that people find personal growth with a family and they also find out a lot about themselves by having a family. When it comes to personal growth, you have to recognize a change in yourself. Sometimes people will grow from having a family and sometimes they won't change at all.

When you begin a family expectedly, you know that there are going to be changes, but you won't realize just what will change and how; you'll have some expected and unexpected change. When you have a family all of a sudden without planning it, you have more personal growth and it comes quickly.

If you are planning a family addition, you have to think about who you are and what you want to be. If you are a type of person who likes to stay out at all hours and party, you may not be ready for the change or the responsibility. When you are giving something like responsibility you change so that you can manage the situation. Sometimes you may feel like you are hitting a wall and you may become overwhelmed, but calm down and let your emotions go.

Once you are able to let go of your emotions, you will know exactly what is expected from you and you will learn and grow. When you have a family, you prepare yourself by thinking about all the good times and rough times that you had with your parents and then you may look back and want to change. How would you feel if your child did the same things that you did? How would you like to be treated like you treated your parents? At that moment, you may become ashamed of who you once where and you may end up finding yourself growing up and settling down.

For those who have an expected family, you grow because you realize that your mother or father was right. You realize that all the things that they did to stop you from having "fun" was just their way of protecting you. As you carry the baby or watch it grow you will find growth by seeking out your parent's support, as well as, carry the knowledge of what a person shouldn't do. With all your life experiences, you learn something. When you have something major like a child on the way, you should reflect and ask yourself "what is the lesson". Then take your experiences and allow yourself to grow and get on a path that will allow you to support and take care of yourself and the baby.

Do you know that most of your growing up will actually be once the baby comes? That's because no one really sees how much commitment goes with having a baby. Then you will also grow and become someone who you never dreamed of being with the support of your family. Your family will help and support you to become a great parent and provider. There are plenty of lessons that you will learn from creating a family, but you can also grow with the help of your parents and family.

Throughout your childhood your parents were always there to guide. They tried to show you the right way to go about life and the wrong way to go about life. Every time you reflect on your actions and compare what the consequences were, you grow. You may have to fall completely on your face to grow up and become a responsible and well adjusted citizen, or you may have to get in a little bit of trouble to see the light. However, everything that we do has consequences and a lesson.

For you to feel personal growth in your career you have to follow the rules for Maslow's Hierarchy of Needs. In this theory you have five needs that always must be present for you to have fulfillment. They are physiological, safety needs, social needs, self actualization, and self esteem. When it comes to your Maslow needs, you will find that you can have a fulfilling life and career, as long as, you can recognize what your needs are.

As for physiological needs, you always have them covered. These needs are the basics of survival and function. You will always have a roof over your head, water and food to consume, and you can satisfy your needs for sleep, sex, and reproduction easily. These needs are never in question; however, all the other needs pertain to your career. Have you ever noticed someone who is irritable after they lose their job? That's because their needs are not being met. They need to have a career to be fulfilled, and this concept involves everyone. For you to feel good about yourself, you have to have a purpose.

Next comes your safety needs. For you to have a career that you can live for, you need to feel safe in your building or place of work. You need to feel free to come and go and you need to feel like you can express yourself. You need to not be threaten to open your ideas up to management or your co-workers, as well as, have physical safety. If you go to work everyday living with a threat to your life, there is no way that you can satisfy your other needs or have a fulfilling career.

Then you have to think about your social needs. Your social needs not only evolve around your work life, but your personal life. Even though you should never mix personal with business, you need to be able to satisfy them both. You need to be able to go to work and find some friends and you also need to have the time after work to have a family, a love life, and a social life outside of your co-workers. You need to have co-works that appreciate and respect you, and then you also need to have people outside of work to support and fulfill your life. These can be very hard to do, especially if you are just starting out and need to put in the extra hours. The more responsibility that you have at work, the more important and difficult your social needs will become.

Then you have to think about your self esteem in the business. You need to think about the things that will make you happy at your job. You need to think about all the things that you want from you career. When it comes to your self esteem, you need to think about getting a promotion, getting a raise, getting some of the benefits of your position or responsibilities. If you can set goals to raise your self esteem in the business setting, you are one step closer to achieving high self esteem. If you don't get the promotion or raise that you were hoping, you will need to go back to social needs and satisfy those that you lack.

Then once you have maintained a good amount of protection, social, and self esteem needs, you are on your way to self actualization. Once you can look at your job or career and tell yourself that you are so proud and satisfied, and then you are at self actualization where you can be content. Even though there are only four steps until you have self actualization, you will find that you may have to repeat some of the stages numerous times before reaching your goal of self actualization.

How to realize your personal growth and your self esteem

Personal growth and self esteem go hand and hand. You have to have self esteem to grow, but sometimes you need to grow to gain self esteem. There are so many things that you can do to keep the two in balance, however, you have to realize that it can very time consuming. You will need to think about the two separately and connected.

First, set some goals. What goals do you really want to do within a specific amount of time? Give yourself at least a month for each goal. Always set your goals realistically or your self esteem will end up diminishing. When you set goals you try to think about how you can get where you want to be. You get creative and grow from all the experiences, regardless of how good or bad the experiences may be.

When you go for something you will have set backs and struggles, but you will learn from all of the struggles and you will grow. Once you have set the goal, you will also find your self esteem rising. You will notice that you walk a little bit taller and that you feel a little bit more confident. The more goals that you met the more your self esteem will rise. Not only will you have higher self esteem, but you will have more success because you have faith in yourself. Self esteem can make you or break you.

When it comes to self esteem, you have to realize just how powerful it can be. You will find that if you go for something and achieve it, you feel like you can do anything, but as soon as you fail, you will begin to think you're worthless and so on. You need to be able to balance your self esteem. You don't want to be in the clouds all the time, but you don't want to be off the charts either. When you achieve something you have to think about all the hard work you put into and how you achieved the goal. This will allow you to grow because you are able to see that you had the power to achieve your goal all the time. Then if you go for something and fail, don't think negatively.

You have to think about why you failed. Learn from the lesson, not just accept your fate. You may not have wanted it as much as someone else or you may not have put your entire heart into. That's okay too. You can go for something and not put your full heart into, however, you have to accept the defeat with grace if you lose. You can grow from your failures. You can look inside yourself and see why you failed and then next time you can fix the problem. Next time, you can either put more effort forth or you can accept a graceful defeat.

If you take the lesson from your experiences and you use them in a positive way, you will be able to grow as a person and you will be able to keep your spirits up. Not only will find that your self esteem will remain, but you will also find that you will continuously grow from all the things that happen to you. If you can take your failures with a grain of salt and look at them objectively you will be able to keep your self esteem up and that will make your success rate higher. You will find that you'll get things done and with efficiency. Look at the little picture, but always keep the bigger picture in mind.

CHAPTER 9- DIFFERENT TYPES OF PERSONALITY AND DEALING WITH EACH

The Attributes of the Controller Personality

A controller is usually someone who takes initiative in doing things naturally. They are the ones who have no problems with decision making. These people appear to be strong-willed, confident, capable and efficient.

When controllers are hanging out with their friends, they will come out with ideas of the activities. They will decide where the places will be and who will be in-charge of a certain task. When a controller is running his own company, he knows exactly which direction to head to. In a family, if a husband is a controller, the wife and children will not need to worry about a thing simply because the husband has already made all the decisions.

This group of people is very task-oriented. Whenever a task is given to them, you can be sure they are in good hands and know they will get it done on time. Their motto is this – no matter what it takes, it has to be done.

How about the sensitive side of them? Well, if you are a lady and looking for a new age sensitive guy, controllers are going to disappoint you.

Controllers appear to be insensitive and emotions will not normally affect them in any way. While some of your friends may not even dare to confront you of your wrongdoings, these people have no problems with it comes to confrontation.

A Controller's Strengths

Get Things Done: A controller's performance is always almost certain. Not only that they get things done right, but also fast and on time. They will use all the resources available and the only thing they want to save is time. Even money is not so much of a big deal when it comes to solving problems.

Remain Calm Under Pressure: Have you seen people who cannot work under pressure? Are you one of them? If you are, controllers can definitely help you to overcome if you model after their character. They remain calm when problems arise and are still able to make rational and wise decisions.

Innovative: Yes, they are innovative. If you put them in the middle of a jungle, they are probably the last ones to starve to death because they will find various ways to keep themselves alive.

If you have heard Air Asia, a budget domestic airline in Malaysia, they are pretty good in innovation. The CEO, Tony Fernandes took over the directorship of the airline while it was still losing money. However, through his innovative creativity, he was able to turn the airlines around. He changed the entire booking system to online and sales started to boost. It has expanded and still expanding ever since. Not only they are routing domestic flights today, they are also operating flights to other countries like Singapore, Indonesia, Macau, England, Australia and New Zealand. Even MAS Airlines (Malaysia Airlines), couldn't keep up with the competition.

I like their motto and it goes like this – We Innovate, Others Imitate!

Recognized Leadership: Since controllers are the ones who start the ball rolling, they are often recognized of their leadership and authorities. Some people call them the born leader, even many leaders are made.

A Controller's Weaknesses

Weak in Support: A controller is usually weak in support. In layman's term, if you are looking for encouragement or support when you are down emotionally, controller is probably the last person you want to go to. You would probably hear from term phrases like, "just face it", "get a life", or "just move on, what's the big deal" and these are the words you do not want to hear when you are down.

Relationships May Not Be Their First Priority: While many of them are married and have children, to some controllers relationships may not be their first priority. Even they may present during your family outing but corporal ideas are spinning in their heads most of the time.

Neglect the Feelings of Others: Don't be surprised if controllers push you too hard in what you do because in their minds, results are all that matter. You may be thinking about having a great night out with your friends and yet at the same time, your boss needs to you to work overtime in order to meet deadlines.

The Attributes of the Promoter Personality

Although controllers are the ones who make decisions for the group or organizations, they may not be the ones who get the most attention at the time. The moment the planning part is done, the controllers" job is also done.

On the other hand, promoter may capture the attention of the public very easily simply because of their promoting nature. They are expressive, keep the crowd entertained, come out with the jokes spontaneously and capture the attention of the people who are present. The things that they say do not even need to make sense.

They appear to be happy, active, outgoing and friendly. Some may even wonder why they can talk and express so well and at the same time, a minority will find him irritating. People generally love to have promoters around because they are not boring and personable.

Who are the examples of a promoter?

• The Mask (acted by Jim Carrey)

• Buddy Love from the Nutty Professor Movie

• Shrek's Donkey

Mr. and Mrs. Personality

Yeah I know they are all fictional characters but I am sure you are able to tell who have got the promoter's attributes among the people around you.

A Promoter's Strengths

People Enjoy Their Presence: If there is one thing that is certain about them, it has to be people's joy to have promoters around. They are just fun to be with and they can talk about just anything on earth.

This is one thing controllers probably need to learn to adapt – to be a more people person regardless of the benefits one gets.

Creative and Imaginative: Not only promoters are able to talk about almost anything on earth; they are able to imagine and express it in a very dramatic ways. That way, people will always enjoy listening to his stories and conducts.

Good Starters: They are often excited with new tasks and love to explore new things in their lives. As a result, they are pretty good in getting good impression for the things that they do for the first few times.

Take Care of the Feelings of Others: Even though they are expressive, they will still take good care of the feelings of others. They will never push too hard even when they jokes about the flaws of the person around.

A Promoter's Weaknesses

Impulsive: You will be surprised with the speed they act that at times, they even act impulsively. Even though they are creative and imaginative, when it comes to problems solving, they are pretty weak.

All they want is stress-free and as a result, they make impulsive decisions with no rational considerations when pressure comes.

Not A Good Finisher: Due to their curiosity nature, they are often excited about new things or tasks. You will find them doing great work when they are just starting and when routine sets in, you will find them settle for the less rather than the best.

They May Act Dramatically: There will be times when they act dramatically to the point it will give you a shock. They would do silly things others people won't and rationalism does not mean anything to them.

Not Paying Attention to Details: If you need them to pay attention to data or details, I would suggest that you look for someone else because they really have no interest in details. They love to make generalization about certain things and often they jump into the conclusion very quickly.

The Attributes of the Analyzer Personality

The analyzers are very feeling-based. Most of the time, they make decision based on their feelings on security. If there is any sense of insecurity, the process will take even longer, simply because they need to gather more data for themselves or the situations.

Data and analysis are extremely important to this group of people. When problem arises, they will take time to study, gather data and analyze the situation with whatever resources available. Not only data and facts, opinions and thoughts of the people involved are also essential to them.

Mr. and Mrs. Personality

Normally analyzers appear to be very academic and tend to be very serious when it comes to working environment. Their conversation maybe based on facts, histories or past illustrations.

Some people may find talking to them boring and at the same time, things that are coming out from their mouth are good to be used for advice.

One of the common examples would include middle-aged staffs that have little interests in the culture change, especially in the company. They are comfortable with where they currently are and risk is just not something they would want on their way. They can be secure yet stubborn.

An Analyzer's Strengths

Sense of Security: This is probably their #1 concern. Their decisions have to be made based on the security for the entire plan. If plan A does not work, plan B has to be ready to work. The data and analysis they use can make the problem solving process to be implemented in the safest way.

Systematic: They love systems and routine is definitely okay for them. The reason being is that, they love to do things in a way that can be followed through from A-Z, preferably without errors. You will gain their favor if the solution you provide can be done systematically.

Risk Management: Risk management is also their greatest strength. When you work with people who will no margin of errors, you will be sure these guys really mean business. Based on the data, opinions and thoughts they have collected, they will manage the risk to the lowest point possible.

Rules and Regulations: Although many people on earth find rules and regulations to be restricting, analyzers work best with rules and regulations. In fact, they can't live without rules and regulations. If the task is set within the boundaries where they can monitor closely, it gives them peace in their hearts.

An Analyzer's Weaknesses

Not Flexible: It is almost impossible for them to adapt new culture. If you are trying to sell the latest accounting software to analyzer, he would tell you a million reasons why he does not need it and how comfortable he is with the one he is using right now. Unless they really see the need of it, otherwise, they would not want to risk it.

Take Too Long to Solve Problems: Just because they need the plan to be perfect before they actually execute it, they will spend a lot of time and effort looking for the right data. Sometimes, it may go longer than what is required and if that happens, the problem may cost them even more resources like money and human labor.

They Do Not Approach Others: Don't find it uncommon when the analyzers do not come and start a conversation with you. It is just in their blood or not their thing to initiate a discussion with others. Even in a brainstorming session, an analyzer will wait for the suggestions and opinions of others to come in first before he actually speaks.

Hidden Emotions: Most of the analyzers hide their emotions simply because they do not want to appear to be weak. Of course there are many reasons why they want to hide their feelings from the public but generally, in order to feel safe and protected, that is the way to go.

The Attributes of the Supporter Personality

Supporters are usually likable and very people-oriented. For promoters, people enjoy a promoter's presence solely because of his ability to entertain. However, people place their trusts on the supporters mainly because of their ability to care, encourage and support.

This is why, when you break up with your boyfriend of 10 years, you wouldn't want to go to a controller or analyzer, but a supporter for comfort.

Since it is their nature to be people-oriented, they tend to avoid personal conflicts in any way possible; even it means to cost the innocence of themselves. It will be really difficult for them to reject people and they will please anyone who comes on their ways (and of course, I am not talking about the criminal kind of demand).

They are also very responsive to people. When people are around, they will usually blend in to the conversation and go with the flow. They let others to initiate any kinds of activities and yet they do not have the interest to impress others.

This is the species that appear to be harmless and non-threatening. Even when they are threatened, they will not make it to the public and some of them suppress their feelings to the point of depression, which is not good at all.

A Supporter's Strengths

Willing to Serve Others: Supporters will have no problems serving the different needs of others. Often, they are the ones who will do the dirty work where many people find it difficult to do.

Accepts Supervision Readily: Supporters are always ready to work under the supervision of their superiors. They are okay with taking commands and do what is required of them.

Others First: Well, I hate to admit this but this is definitely something which you will never find in me. The amazing thing about the supporters is that, they usually place their importance below others.

It is not that they have a sense of inadequacy, but it is really their nature to put people first regardless of any incentives or rewards in return.

Good for Encouragement: If you are looking for a listener so that you can pour out all your feelings that have been hidden for a long time, they are the source to go. You will be amazed with their patience and how encouraged you can be right after you talk to them.

A Supporter's Weaknesses

Withhold Unpleasant Information: If you happen to see your best friend's husband to be holding another's girl hand in a shopping mall, would you have the courage the tell her of the incident?

This is probably one of the greatest setbacks a supporter has. They withhold unpleasant information simply they do not want to see you heartbreak.

Tendency to Please Everybody: There is a saying that goes like this, "I do not know the secrets to succeed, but I know secrets to fail is trying to please everybody". When we are making major decisions, there will always be people who go against it and for supporters; they will have hard time understand this.

Lack Interest in Planning: Supporters are probably not born for planning and goal setting. Controllers can make good use of supporters to help in execution of the plans because they submit to their authorities but really, planning and goal-setting is not their thing.

The Attributes of the Promoter/Supporter Personality

Basically, the promoter/supporter personality is the mixture of promoter and supporter personalities. A promoter may be fun to hang out with but it does not mean he has genuine friendships at all. The same goes to a supporter – one does not need to capture the attention of the crowd in order to have a lot of genuine friendships.

What happens to the promoter/supporter personality then? It is simply referring to a person who is very expressive in things that he does and at the same time, he values the relationships and people around him.

This kind of people uses their charisma to build relationships with the people around him. Even though they appear to be the star in the crowd, relationships with people is definitely a big thing to him.

While promoters may only value their own opinions, in the promoter/supporter personality, a person values both his own and the ideas of others. This kind of people can be more appealing simply because of the hidden strength they have.

A Promoter/Supporter's Strength

Appear to be Charismatic: A person with charisma does not usually need any makeup or pretend to be others in other to gain acceptance from the people around him. Charisma is really an aura that will attract the attention of the majority the moment he starts to talk and act.

Love to Laughs: Due to the fact that a supporter may not laugh all the time, the promoter/supporter personality allows the person to enjoy laughing. Even when tough situations come, he is still able to laugh and make fun of it. With this, he will definitely make the atmosphere to be less tensed.

Make The Journey Enjoyable: If you can find a person who can journey with you and make you laugh throughout the entire journey, wouldn't it be nice? This is the ability of a promoter/supporter person. Not only he is able to make the environment around him enjoyable but also he is the one who will value the friendships with the people.

A Promoter/Supporter's Weaknesses

Stand Strong For Both Himself and Others: When a person values both his and the opinions of others, he places himself into a conflict of opinions. For a pure promoter, he values his own opinions. On the other hand, a supporter values the opinions of others. When the two clashes – in the promoter/supporter personality, the person can get himself into a serious argument in order to stand up for his thoughts.

Can't Handle Details: Don't bother looking for a person with a promoter/supporter personality to work on details. They are just not for it due to their nature.

Can't Work Under Pressure: They may be the star in the crowd and value good relationships but when they are dealing with stress, they really can't perform. Since they are best to work under authority, giving them specific instructions can definitely help in getting to job done effectively.

The Attributes of the Promoter/Controller Personality

A person with promoter/controller personality is normally expressive in an aggressive way. Unlike promoter/supporter, relationships may not matter to them but success and sense of achievement can be a really big thing to them.

Now, a controller may be achieving great success but still remains a low profile. I personally know a person who has been declared bankruptcy and yet he owns a company that makes millions of dollars in profit yearly. On the other hand, promoter/controller can be achieving great success at the same time, but the fact that he is rich and successful is made known to all over the world.

This group of people love challenges and always strives to win. Not just to win, but to win with flying colors. It is not quite common for them to stay in the same position for long. They need to jump from one place to another.

Stagnancy will just bore them and they chase their goals and dreams with intensity.

In terms of conversations, they are the ones who dominate. People listen to them the moment they speak and their voices turn out to be clearly visible. In addition, speeches that they make will usually carry much weight.

A Promoter/Controller's Strengths

Absolutely No Problems with Unfamiliarity: A promoter/controller will have no problems with unfamiliarity. Even they are new to the environment, their promoter nature will just help them to get along with people very well.

When it comes to something new, there is no such word as „uncomfortable" in their dictionaries. With their controller personality, they are able to see their goals bigger than anything else that is on their ways.

Independent: You may find it strange but a promoter/controller is extremely independent. Many people work for the sake of their families. Some work for some other purposes. Promoters/controllers work for their own sake. Their strong will and power strive them to constantly stay at the top notch in what they are doing.

Decisive: While a pure promoter may not be decisive, a promoter/controller is expert in decision making. Not only they are fast but they are also accurate in relation to their judgment.

A Promoter/Controller's Weaknesses

Profile May Result in Threats: When your success has been made known to the public by own luxurious cars, a valley and a yacht, the tendency of you being threatened are much higher. Some of the unethical competitors or peers are going to eat you up without your acknowledge. They do not rejoice in seeing you succeed but stumble and fall. I am not saying you cannot buy luxurious cars, a valley or yacht but you just need to be careful because there are people out there who love to see you fail.

No Space for Others: Very often, promoters/controllers are the ones who do most of the talking. Hence, it leaves no space for their peers to express their suggestions and opinions. They probably need to learn to allow others to access to their lives or discussions.

Lack of Patience: You just can't help it but promoters/controllers act very quickly that they want to get things done quickly even sometimes without the need of gathering the complete resources.

Produce Stressful Subordinates: Sometimes, their subordinates or staffs will have hard time working with the promoters/controllers simply because of their fast moving nature. As a result, staffs are dying to meet deadlines and work under intensive pressures.

The Attributes of the Controller/Analyzer Personality

The first thing that comes to my mind in relation to the controller/analyzer personality is this – they are stiff! I am not sure if it is the right word to describe them but to me, they are probably the last person on earth I would want to hang out with. Unless it is required, there will be no way I'd want to meet them.

Anyway, let's talk about the controllers/analyzers. They are efficient and business-minded. Apart from getting desired results, they are also keen in gathering information. Even sometimes the implementation of the plan may take much longer than required, nevertheless the probability of the success is almost guaranteed.

This group of people is not so good in placing their trusts on others. They can be very critical and judgmental to the point that they only place their trusts on the people who have been working effectively for them in the past. Any first timers will have to perform extremely well in order to gain the initial favor of the controllers/analyzers.

Needless to say, they are very task-oriented. They are not driven by emotions and often very rational when it comes to making decisions. They are calm and steady even the biggest obstacles set in. No matter what, they will get it done.

Finally, it is normal to them so scan through the situation or a person who is in front of them. They will generate all kinds of perceptions, data and judgment on the situations and person, causing the person especially to panic easily.

A Controller/Analyzer's Strengths

Tasks Are Organized: You just can't go wrong under the supervision of the controllers/analyzers. Their tasks are organized in a very systematic manner. They know exactly what and where went wrong when any part of the planning process fails.

Seen as Honored: Controllers/Analyzers earn their respects due to their experiences and abilities to solve complicated problems. They can be very good advisors and rationality always go with them in things that they do.

Results Are Almost Certain: With the information controllers/analyzers gather, it is almost certain they will produce excellent results. These are the people who are highly demanded in the business industries.

A Controller/Analyzer's Weaknesses

Avoid Working With Others: While it is impossible to get things done all by themselves, they are very critical with the people they choose to work with. Unless you have already shown your efficiency in the past, it is really hard for them to involve you as a part of their team.

Not People-Oriented: Relationships with others do not mean a lot to them and hence, lack passionate and understanding. They may think it is okay to spend the weekend in the office and at the same time, their staffs may think weekend is the only time they can spend with their family members.

Appear Distant: Most of the time, they are seen distant and isolated from the crowd. The topics in their conversation are nothing more than the tasks and data. Talking about the weather or how well your children are doing at schools will not interest them all at. Also, some people find them difficult to relate.

Judgmental: Due to their analytical nature, they can be very judgmental even if they do not know you too well. However, time may have the potential to reveal the person's character further.

The Attributes of the Analyzer/Supporter Personality

The group of analyzers/supporters is rather interesting. Even relationships may matter to them; they will always struggle to develop genuine friendships simply because of their analyzer nature as well.

For instance, they may long for friendships and at the same time, they are also critical when it comes to choosing the right friends.

As a result, they rarely initiate conversations in interpersonal situations. They will usually wait for others to approach them or let others to voice out their opinions before they speak their very first word in the conversation.

They can be of very good support yet analytical. Time is needed for them to place their trust fully on a person.

An Analyzer/Supporter's Strengths

Harmonic With Others: They are very harmonic with others. No signs of threats or harms are seen in them and they get along pretty well with others.

Good As Counselor: With their analytical experiences, you can definitely rely on them for advice. Since they are the analyzers/supporters, they have no problems with giving you advice and better still, analyze the situation so that you can have the best solution to the problems.

Choose the Right Words to Say: This is a skill you probably won't find on the other personalities. Although they may have opinions about you die to their analytical nature, they will also choose the right way or words to deliver to you simple because they do not want to hurt you, based on their supporter's nature.

Choose Friends Carefully: They may appear to be friends to many people. However, not many are close to them. They choose friends very carefully and only allow friends to gain access to their personal lives when deep trusts are developed.

An Analyzer/Supporter's Weaknesses

Hesitant to Voice Out an Opinion: It is difficult to ask of their honest opinions. They are careful when dealing with feelings of others and sometimes, they choose not to disclose certain unpleasant information just to protect the heart of the intended person.

Conflicts of Valuing Analysis and Friendship: This kind of conflict is complicated and it happens when the analytical nature sabotage the purpose of a friendship. For instance, there will be times when you keep gathering the data of your good friend – his behaviors and the way he talks. Too much of this will defeat the purpose of a friendship. Which one do you actually value the most? The data gathered or the friendship?

The Attributes of the Centric Personality

Now, I would say the people with the centric personality are almost perfect. They use the right approach to communicate, depending on who they are talking to. When they are talking to controllers, they switch their mode to relate to the controllers. When people come to them for support, they become compassionate with the feelings of the broken-hearted.

Isn't it amazing if we have the centric personality?

Even they are strong-willed, they do not appear to be manipulative. Even when they are supporting, they do not try to withhold unpleasant information from the intended person. In fact, they choose the correct way to deliver the bad news to the person.

In the working environment, they can probably get along well with both superiors and also subordinates. Bosses love them and staffs are happy to work under them.

Seriously, they appear to be flawless and people with centric personality are usually the most charismatic leaders you could possibly find on earth.

A Centric's Strength

Flexible: They are flexible. They have no problems with changes and can adapt to the new environments very quickly. When building relationships, they do not need to take long to gather useful information.

In fact, they can get along with each of the personality group pretty well. Not even the controller/analyzer can stop them from giving their best performance.

A Charismatic Leader: The moment a centric speaks, the entire world will listen to him. He simply knows what he is talking about and doing. He celebrates when he does things right and admits his mistakes when he makes wrong decisions. They are usually transparent and it is almost impossible to find character flaws in them.

Able to Relate to Different Types of People: You may be talking to a centric about the liquor you had in the party last night and he feels excited about it. On the next day, you will be surprised to see him being able to impress his stuffy boss to implement the plan he suggested for the company. No matter where the centric are, they are able to relate to different types of people.

A Centric's Weaknesses

Hard to Predict: I am not sure if this is the weakness but it is often hard to predict the behavior of a centric. You wouldn't be able to read his mind normally. In one side, they are smart. However, if they are placed in the wrong hands or exist for the purpose of ill-wills, the centric may become a tricky wolf that will eat you up.

ABOUT THE AUTHOR

Alvin Harper is a teacher and is currently pursuing his studies in psychology. His main goal in life is to help as many people as he could by inspiring them and by always instilling in their minds that there is always a way and hope in every circumstances that they may in, no matter how messy it gets.

Understanding one's personality is a crucial key on how to proceed in life with a great percentage of success.

Alvin lives in Nebraska with his family.

www.ingramcontent.com/pod-product-compliance
Lightning Source LLC
Chambersburg PA
CBHW050648250726
48662CB00002B/562